MG

Foulis

Haynes

Titles in the Foulis Mini Marque History series:

AC
Alfa Romeo
Ferrari
Jaguar
Lotus
MG
Porsche (in preparation)
Rolls-royce

Further titles will be published on a regular basis. For information on new titles contact your bookseller or write to the publishers.

ISBN 0 85429 229 2

First published January 1979
Reprinted 1980, 1982

A FOULIS Motoring Book

Haynes Publishing Group
Sparkford, Yeovil, Somerset BA22 7JJ, England

Distributed in North America by:
Haynes Publications Inc.
861 Lawrence Drive, Newbury Park, California 91320 USA

Editor: Rod Grainger
Layout design: Simon Slade
Cover design: Phill Jennings
Cover photo: 1939 MG TB Owned by Mr. T. Newbold of Tollerton.
       (Courtesy Tony Evans)
Printed by: J. H. Haynes & Co. Ltd, Sparkford, Yeovil, Somerset BA22 7JJ

CONTENTS

To Brian and Shirley Warren ... and Smelly Ellie, the cat.

AUTHOR'S INTRODUCTION

For many many years, MG has been the greatest name in British sports cars. Brief to an extreme, but symbolic of a whole concept, those two initials have come to be synonymous with the very term *sports car* to the public at large, whether they be motoring enthusiasts or housewives; whether they be British, European or American. Indeed, in the USA MG cars had an impact, and a cult following, which could never have been imagined by founder, Cecil Kimber, and his band of highly enthusiastic craftsmen at the MG factory in Abingdon.

Abingdon-on-Thames, as the once sleepy river-side town is known in full, became the home of MG in 1929 and had little chance of remaining sleepy after that! Such was the spirit and success of the marque that, while MGs were delighting both owners and spectators alike on road and track, it was even being suggested that the cows in Abingdon left octagonal hoof marks!

Financed initially by the great William Morris, based originally on Morris production units of a more 'shopping' nature and created by the leadership and determination of Cecil Kimber, the MG marque has a long and illustrious story. Early breakthroughs, subsequent failures, a seemingly endless succession of varied models, a neat little sideline in world record breaking, the application of much more rigid business principles under Leonard Lord and the enormous success of post-war MGs - all are described within these pages. So, too, the MG 'magic' and its sad erosion subsequent to the take-overs and mergers of the late sixties and seventies.

What this book attempts to do is describe MG's history in both chronological order and readable fashion. In being comprehensive, I have also had, necessarily, to be brief in many instances, but have tried to present the facts in the fairest manner. Whereas the greater part of the story lends itself to many superlatives, the seventies have introduced a somewhat dull and barren chapter to dampen the old MG spirit. Thanks to the intricacies and rationalisation of big business and mass production, the two famous initials seem to have lost their way somewhere in the corridors of British Leyland.

Leaving the story on a sad note isn't the most satisfactory situation, but at least one knows there are many more chapters to come in the future. Let us hope they can describe a more ambitious approach from Abingdon, the rekindling of the spirit and an exciting new model to generate some fresh MG 'magic'.

Peter Filby
Redhill, Surrey
November, 1978

MR. MORRIS MEETS MR. KIMBER

William Richard Morris was born at Worcester on the 10th of October 1877. Little more than a decade later a fellow called Cecil Kimber came into this world at Dulwich, South-East London. Had these two men's paths not crossed in 1921 our planet would have been deprived of what was to become a universally accepted household name - that of MG. The fact that those two letters are synonymous with the term 'sports car' to the public at large, whether they be motoring enthusiasts or surburban housewives, is almost entirely due to Kimber, for he *was* MG. But the marque's incredible growth would scarcely have been possible without the agreement, assistance and finance of companies belonging to Morris.

As a very young child, William Morris lived on his mother's family farm at Headington, Oxford. He could hardly have guessed that much of the area would later become littered with a sprawling motor car manufacturing complex of which control would be his. There could have been no inkling that henceforth one of the world's greatest automobile engineering empires would stand across the very sites of his father's grammar school and his own village school, both at nearby Cowley. Remarkable too, that the headmaster's parlour of his father's school was eventually to be retained as Morris' office, perhaps with a touch of sentimentality. Yet, from small beginnings that young boy became Lord Nuffield, his name a legend, his industrial achievements brilliant, and his products, more especially those bearing the famous octagonal badge, giving endless pleasure to millions.

After emigrating to America, Morris' father Frederick had for some time driven a mail coach in Winnipeg, Canada. Following this early family association with wheels, a youthful W.R.M. (as he later came to be known)

left school at sixteen and continued the theme in becoming apprenticed to an Oxford bicycle maker. Some nine months later he had already saved enough to open his own bicycle repair and servicing business. These early stages of a remarkable career were given further momentum when the determined and clever engineer began to produce his own Morris bicycle. Dedication and hard work soon saw the business flourish. With the twentieth century in its tenderest years, W.R.M. would often be called from his workshop in Longwall Street, Oxford to assist the city's earliest automobilists - at least, those whose noisy, smelly and often frightening projectiles had come to some sort of mechanical grief. Very soon, The Oxford Garage, as the Longwall Street premises were known, played host to the development of the very first Morris motor-cycle, built with a strengthened cycle frame and wheels,

Far and away the most popular MG of all time, the MGB was introduced in 1962 and is nowadays selling better than ever. Little could Cecil Kimber have guessed ...

and powered by a Morris-constructed engine. It was the prototype of a production series that established W.R.M. as a manufacturer of reliable motor-cycles, and gave him the essential engineering experience necessary before the next vital steps forward could be taken.

The Morris motor-cycle's later use of a de Dion engine invariably linked W.R.M. with early automobiles that used the same power unit. It was a useful warning of the motoring movement's impending spread. By 1908 the Morris motor-cycle manufacturing rights had been disposed of to a friend, and several business ventures now encouraged W.R.M's growing relationship with four-wheeled

9

Early days at Longwall Street, when
William Morris would sell and repair all
manner of used cars and motor cycles

His achievements in the motor industry
brought William Morris first a
knighthood, then a peerage

transport. At Longwall Street, the seeds of a vast empire were germinating more busily than ever, selling and repairing all manner of used cars and motorcycles. Around 1910 further prosperity arrived via new car transactions. The motor car was very definitely booming, and not unnaturally, Morris investigated the possibility of interpreting it in his own fashion. The first stage involved discussions with carburettor manufacturers White and Poppe of Coventry regarding the manufacture of a small car engine to Morris design.

Several thousand pounds working capital was the next hurdle. Not an insurmountable one, though, for it was methodically raised by one of White and Poppe's wholesale agents who, on Morris' behalf, took cash deposits from the motor trade in the course of his travels. Such was progress that W.R.M. rebuilt the old Longwall Street stables and reopened them as The Morris Garage in 1911. It was here, late in 1912, that a new company, W.R.M. Motors Ltd., produced the very first Morris, the Morris-Oxford light car. Sited in the simple chassis frame was a four cylinder 10hp White and Poppe engine with gearbox giving three forward speeds. There was a multiple disc clutch, worm driven rear axle, and suspension of half-elliptic leaf springs front and three-quarter elliptics rear. Headed by a polished brass Bullnose radiator, the Morris-designed two seater body was upright, shapely and coach-built by Raworth Ltd. of Oxford. Here, at least, was the forerunner of the type of vehicle which instigated the MG marque.

The Morris-Oxford light car wasn't a runner until early 1913, the same year in which W.R.M. acquired additional premises to make his sales and repair concern's title plural - The Morris Garages. Simultaneously, he found further premises taking in his father Frederick's old school in nearby Cowley, and it was here that W.R.M. Motors Ltd., embarked upon Morris-Oxford production, thanks to a firm order from Gordon Stewart of car distributors Stewart and Ardern of London. The Oxford quickly caught on. It soon indicated its sporting aspirations, too, and accordingly several coachwork options, including a sporting single-seater, were hurriedly listed.

From humble beginnings, W.R.M. now operated his two businesses, The Morris Garages and W.R.M. Motors Ltd., completely independently. When the first World War hit Britain in 1914, the Cowley works were commandeered for the production of war materials to aid the Allies' victory. Morris, however, still found the off-duty time to organise a handful of men in car production. The result was the appearance early in 1915 of the first Morris Cowley, a cheap economy version of the Oxford to help devour some of the multitude of White and Poppe engines that were lying about the works. Naturally, the now traditional Morris bullnose radiator shape was retained.

By the war's end in 1918 an enormous quantity of war materials had spewed forth from the Cowley works. To cope with production, the premises had been extended out towards the Berkshire hills - the first expansion towards what would later become one of the largest industrial centres in the world, and sadly ruin the surrounding countryside. As motor car construction returned in earnest, the Morris empire reverted to its earlier growth pattern. There had already been some effort applied to the discovery of an alternative source of engines, for at the outbreak of war

The MG marque's earliest ancestor was William Morris' first production car, the 'Bullnose' Morris Oxford

W.R.M. had visited the Continental Motor Manufacturing Company of Detroit in the USA and had agreed to buy 1500 Red Seal engines. In addition, a great many components had been ordered from other American factories. Planned to propel the Cowley, fewer than two thirds of the Red Seal engines ever reached Britain thanks to the great interest shown in Allied merchant ships by enemy submarines. However, when the Western world returned to acting humanely once more, Continental readily sold the Red Seal engine drawings, tools, and components to W.R.M., who found the French armament manufacturers, Hotchkiss, willing to take on production of the design in their British workshops at Coventry. Working for

Hotchkiss at this time was a young engineer named Leonard Lord.

In 1919 W.R.M. Motors Ltd. was renamed Morris Motors Ltd. With production of the Oxford and Cowley models progressing busily as ever at the Cowley factory, and his small group of retail and repair garages proving just as worthwhile, Morris made a crucial decision - a general manager was needed for the latter. The position was filled by Edward Armstead early that year. Before long, a sales manager would be needed too, an appointment that would lead Morris Garages into motoring history.

Cecil Kimber was born on the 12th April 1888. His family had been involved in the printed word and the composition thereof - more recently, his father was a manufacturer of printing equipment. Upon leaving Stockport Grammar School, the young Kimber entered a later branch of the family business which produced

Cecil Kimber's leadership and guidance took MG from the tiniest beginnings to household name status. This picture was taken in his office at Abingdon

The combination of William Morris' business acumen and Cecil Kimber's forceful personality was to produce a remarkable series of MGs. This gathering was photographed in the 1970s

printing ink in Lancashire. But it was things mechanical which really caught the teenage Kimber's mind and, at a time when William Morris was already building his own motor-cycles, Cecil at last purchased his own machine, a second-hand 1906 Rex. Very soon a competitive element had entered his hobby. The consequences were a rapid and appreciative knowledge of the machine's construction and moving parts, plus its replacement by a faster model.

As luck would have it, Kimber and motorcycle met with an untimely accident that damaged both rather severely. Hospital, crutches, operations, and the near loss of his entire right leg plagued Kimber for some two years afterwards. Thankfully, the leg was retained although the injuries had left the young man with an unmatched pair that would force him to limp for the rest of his life. The accident's only positive result was the award of several hundred pounds damages, a portion of which bought a 1913 Singer 10, Kimber's first four-wheeled conveyance. Rapid conveyance might be a more suitable description, for the desire for performance remained strong as ever. Indeed, the greatest part of Kimber's engineering interest now involved the automobile. It was this love and the decline of the family printing ink business that eventually caused enough friction between father and son for the former's lips to remain sealed upon every future meeting of the two.

Cut out of his father's life despite regular attempts to heal the breach, Cecil Kimber followed his convictions. Comparatively late in life, considering his twenty-seven years, he made the important break, with surprising confidence, and joined respected luxury motor car manufacturers Sheffield-Simplex of Yorkshire. Here, at last, his great enthusiasm and irrepressible personality began to show. Yet he found a subservient role came only with difficulty, and 1916 saw him employed by A.C. Cars of Thames Ditton, Surrey. Two years later, Kimber moved again - to transmission unit, axle, and steering assembly suppliers (to William Morris amongst others) E.G. Wrigley Ltd. of Birmingham. Thus his motor business experience grew rapidly, not unnaturally with a distinct sporting edge. When the industry began to shrink from its post-war boom, Wrigley's were amongst those afflicted. Maybe with foresight, possibly with luck, Kimber found further employment with a man who had cleverly turned the collapse to his advantage - William Morris.

Gauging the motor industry storm with skill, Morris Motors Ltd. had wisely elected to reduce their prices, consequently bringing about an appreciable increase in sales. The Morris Garages had likewise suffered negligibly, and it was to one of the group's garages that in 1921 Cecil Kimber first went as sales manager. As fate would have it, the group's general manager Edward Armstead resigned early in 1922, and Kimber needed no second thoughts when offered the position. Thus this ambitious man had reached a position of some responsibility after only a few years in the business. It was some measure of what was soon to follow, particularly as Kimber's sporting aspirations could at last be explored in more depth. With this driving, forceful personality now under the wing of the great, and equally ambitious, W.R.M. (Morris Motors had already produced something like 30,000 Oxfords and Cowleys), the first vital link had been made in the establishment of what would become the MG legend.

EARLY DAYS AT MORRIS GARAGES

Despite his great enthusiasm for and keen progress in the motor car business, Cecil Kimber did not possess outstanding engineering skill. Regarded more as a practical engineer, and even then not by all his associates, he was better noted for his organisational ability. Upon becoming General Manager of the Morris Garages early in 1922, he was able to develop his creative thinking whilst attending to the day-to-day tasks of handling the group's retail dealings.

The Morris Garages were happily the leading group of retail and repair garages in Oxford. For some time the company had sold a variable range of special equipment for Morris cars, and had also been concerned with the preparation of more sporting chariots, both motorcycles and cars. With customers appearing from all over Oxfordshire there was no shortage of sporting interest, and a competitive spirit had no doubt already developed amongst the employees. Indeed, Morris himself had not been shy of healthy competition. In the early days he'd publicised his first bicycles by becoming a local cycling champion. This had led to successful competitive outings on his Morris motorcycles and, during the earliest days of Morris car construction, his participation in several motor car hillclimbs and long distance trials.

Although Morris had warmed to the thrill of competition in those early days, his fascination was not to last. Modified versions of his cars were raced, but the marque would always be essentially a practical conveyance. This 'shopping' nature was reflected in the strain of solid and reliable motor car that The Morris Garages sold and repaired - Belsize, Hupmobile, Singer, Standard and Wolseley, plus of course the Morrises Oxford and Cowley. Both sports versions and two-seater open versions of the Morrises were available on the standard chassis, but the truly functional 'sports car' had not yet arrived on the motoring scene. Bearing in mind his growing sporting aspirations, Cecil Kimber can hardly have been greatly excited by the cars that sat in his showrooms. He resolved to apply a little creativity. As though the job of running The Morris Garages was not enough, much of his spare time was now employed with the design and drawing of special bodies that could be fitted to the standard Morris chassis.

Morris Motors Ltd. already offered a wide variety of body styles on their standard chassis. Early bodywork had been produced first by Raworth of Oxford, then by Hollick & Pratt of Coventry. His earlier interest in competition now evaporating, William Morris was only occasionally taken to a slice of sporting fun with spartan, special-bodied Morrises. Of the several built, one was particularly intriguing. Shaped like a boat, it was constructed from thin strips of wood alternately stained to produce a strange and startling effect. With polished aluminium bonnet, discs over

The 11.9hp Morris Cowley model provided the chassis and mechanical basis for Morris Garages' first products

the spoked wheels and nickel-plated brightwork, it was a fascinating machine that W.R.M. enjoyed immensely, though treated as strictly a specialist one-off.

Undeterred by Morris' views, soon after assuming his promoted position at Morris Garages, Kimber persuaded Morris Motors at Cowley to supply Cowley chassis which he planned to clothe with a sporting-type body of his own design. As opposed to the usual two-seater with 'dickey' arrangement, in which the folding hood left the two 'dickey' passengers to fend for themselves whatever the weather, Kimber plumped for a more considerate 'Chummy' style. This at least brought the two occasional rear seat passengers within the hood's protection. Chosen as most suitable of the half-dozen Morris Garages' premises spread around Oxford, the main service depot at the old Longwall Street workshops now played host to the construction of the first batch of Morris Garages Chummy models. Produced by a small group of men (including one notable man, Cecil Cousins, who had joined the Company as a cycle shop fitter in 1920), the Chummy's special body was complemented by rear spring doctoring to lower the Cowley chassis' high back

end, leather upholstery and pastel-coloured paintwork - perhaps setting a precedent for sporting cars of the future.

Propelled by an 11.9hp Hotchkiss engine (as used in standard Morris Motors products), fronted by a traditional Morris bullnose radiator and given purpose by a sloping bonnet with slightly raked windscreen, the Chummy was indeed attractive. It found ready customers, too. Very soon the albeit limited production required small workshops of its own. In summer 1922 a tiny mews garage was found in Alfred Lane, Oxford, and production transferred there into the capable hands of Cecil Cousins, plus assistants. With remarkable devotion, and no doubt inspired by Kimber, the men were soon turning out several Morris Garages cars every week. It was one of these Chummies, modified at Longwall Street, that Kimber himself drove in the London to Lands End Trial long distance event in March 1923, and drove well enough to qualify for a gold medal award for an unpenalised run. This was a small but important success that could only have encouraged Kimber's belief in his work.

His sporting aspirations and creative instincts at last becoming reality in automobile terms, Morris Garages' general manager was embarking on an incredible course of motoring history. But it's at this point in past accounts of the MG story that conflict has reared a confused head. This hasn't exactly been assisted by the fact that the company's business was so scattered about the various Oxford premises that staff at one depot could never be quite sure of what was happening at another. Distinguishing themselves clearly from the Cowley-produced Morris Motors vehicles, Kimber's Chummies were already of a separate identity. Despite being straightforward, special-bodied Morris Cowleys, they embodied an easily recognisable sporting flavour. Whether they were simply Morris Garages cars or could now be called MGs is open to interpretation, though Cecil Cousins was certainly waiting for the next Morris Garages product to appear before he freely applied the MG label. In the mists of time Kimber, it seems, was even more patient.

Quite possibly the London to Lands End Trial success showed a green light for Kimber's next intended project, and prompted its increased sporting flavour. Kimber had designed a lightweight roadster-type two seater body, and ordered six examples from Charles Raworth of Oxford. First appearing in mid-1923, these Morris Garages Raworth sports cars were based on the same modified Cowley chassis as their Chummy predecessors. Both inside and out, the spartan sportsters were well suited to what was then termed a more 'furious' style of driving! Strangely enough, in those days 'furious' meant 60mph, the sort of maximum speed of which the Raworth was capable, despite its somewhat over-enthusiastic Smiths 80mph speedometer. These cars, again, used 11.9hp, 1548cc Hotchkiss engines under their bullnose-fronted bonnets. Other features were a lowered steering column to clear the new dashboard, a raked windscreen, two marine-type ventilator cowls on the scuttle, an absence of front brakes (9 inch drums were fitted to the rear only), and a price of £350. This figure was fairly high considering the Raworth's simple mechanical basis, and this was reflected by the whole year it took to sell the six cars. If, as Cecil Cousins was inclined to think, this was the true birth of the MG marque, it was a meagre one, for sure.

Produced in 1924 and 1925, Cecil Kimber's rebodied version of the 14/28 Morris Oxford chassis has been the subject of some confusion over whether or not it was a true MG

The Raworth's arrival had not interrupted Morris Garages' production of the Chummy. This, however, was precisely the effect achieved by Morris Motors' announcement in 1923 of their Occasional Four 'chummy' model of almost exactly the same specification and appearance, but a significantly lower price. Several hundred Morris Garages Chummies had been built at Alfred Lane by now, but quite obviously all future versions, copies or not, would be supplied by William Morris' ever-expanding Cowley factory. Indeed, Morris Motors Ltd. were striding gaily forwards with quickly widening steps. The company had found such success with their Hotchkiss powered Morrises that

they'd bought up the Coventry engine manufacturers lock, stock and barrel. In doing this, they'd also acquired the services of Hotchkiss employee, Leonard Lord, the consequence of which Morris could hardly have foreseen. Managing Director of Morris Motors Ltd. by 1933, Lord was also to become Managing Director of the MG Car Company Ltd. in 1935 when it was sold to the former. And the consequences of that transaction were far-reaching to an extreme.

In 1923 the big Morris advance was in top gear. Having bought Hotchkiss, W.R.M. next acquired body builders Hollick & Pratt, and neatly extinguished any ideas L.F. Pratt Esq. had of supplying further sporting bodies to Morris Motors. The quickly expanding company was aiming pointedly at the mass production market for what were distinguishable as more practical cars even then. The trend was further supported when later that year they dropped the standard Morris Cowley sporting body from their still varied range of body styles.

The Morris Motors Occasional Four 'chummy' model rather knocked off balance Morris Garages' and Cecil Kimber's settled production of their own Chummy model. Several counter-measures were tried, using as a basis the Morris Oxford chassis - rather than the Cowley chassis as before. But for a time the solution eluded even the inventive Kimber. Saloon, landaulette, coupé and cabriolet - diverse body styles all, but none heralded a brighter future. However, the fact that the more powerful 13.9hp engined Oxford chassis had entered the scene was to be of some further significance, particularly when Kimber was able to study, early in 1924, another manufacturer's open touring conversion of that same chassis - the 14/28 Oxford chassis was its correct title. Its four-seater aluminium body highly polished, its steering column lowered, its suspension modified, this particular conversion directly inspired Kimber's next effort, the Morris Garage Special 4-seater Sports. Advertised at £395, this model was soon succeeded by an improved version of greatly enhanced appearance. Discs covered the spoked artillery wheels, the polished aluminium body was lower, the wings painted blue, scuttle ventilators fitted, both steering and windscreen raked and, naturally, the springs flattened. Fronted by the standard Morris-type bullnose radiator, this handsome machine was sold to Billy Cooper, a well known trials competitor. In his hands, it was soon receiving just the publicity that Kimber needed.

So Morris Garages' car production at Longwall Street and Alfred

Polished aluminium bodywork and disc wheels made the early 14/28 Super Sports MGs look most impressive

Lane had turned to using modified versions of the 13.9hp Oxford chassis. The company was not averse to using perfectly standard Oxford chassis, and did this on more than one occasion. Both chassis variants were graced with various body styles to the buyer's option, but unfortunately few cars were being sold. Only the Special 4-seater Sports open tourer, and its handful of sisters, had received any acclaim, but none of these cars warranted regular production - most certainly not along the lines of the previously successful Morris Garages Chummy. In truth, the Morris Motors Occasional Four had deeply undermined Kimber's calculations. No longer were specialised body cosmetics on a slightly modified standard chassis enough to remain ahead of the competition. If limited production cars were to maintain that slight advantage over the mass producers, the matter of chassis tuning would have to be further explored. Thus, Morris Garages were drawn into the generating of a rapid growth sports car market. The true sports car was close to becoming reality.

Springtime 1924 had found Morris Garages' car constructors beginning work on one noteworthy vehicle that was to cause future historians all manner of headaches when trying to sort out the first generation MGs. Despite the existence of all previous Morris Garages products, including the Raworth open two seaters that Cecil Cousins regarded as the first true MGs, the new car was soon to become known as 'Old Number One'! All very inconsiderate, especially as the 1923/4 Morris Garages Raworth was, in a May 1924 advertisement, referred to as the 'MG' Super Sports Morris. Furthermore, a 1928 booklet produced by the company stated that MG sports cars were first introduced in 1923. Maybe Cousins' views were therefore justified. Kimber, however, is reputed to have regarded 'Old Number One' as the first *proper* MG, despite its failure to be completed until March 1925.

To add to the confusion, both Billy Cooper's Special 4-seater Sports tourer and its predecessor had, along with several other Kimber products, been sometimes advertised as MGs, presumably at Kimber's direction. Certain publications, meanwhile, independently chose to call the cars specially-bodied Morrises which, of course, all Morris Garages products were! In reality, the process was gradual; the MG evolved from the Morris; there was not necessarily a clearly defined dividing line between the two marques at first.

While the slow, year-long construction of 'Old Number One' was taking place, Kimber's cars were steadily growing in stature. It should be mentioned here that Morris Garages advertisements, if not the cars, displayed for the first time in May 1924 the stylised, octagon-enclosed MG motif that is still with us today. It was to be some time, however, before Kimber's attractive corporate image was to be seen on the radiators of his cars. For the time being the bullnose radiators would have to be content with the Morris Garages medallion - the Oxford City crest (depicting an ox crossing the River Thames at a ford) surrounded by a garter bearing the inscription 'The Morris Garages Ltd.'. What with Ox-fords, Cow-leys and Bull-noses, the poor cars could have been excused for being agricultural had they so wished.

But they weren't. Indeed, their stature was moving ever onwards that year with the autumn announcement of the new MG Super Sports Model

range. The specification and construction of these cars were developments on the theme set by Billy Cooper's Special 4-seater Sports open tourer. The same 13.9hp engined Oxford chassis was used, but, as Morris Motors now made it with both 8ft.6in. and 9ft. wheelbases, Kimber chose to put his new open four seater body on the longer chassis, and his two seater variant on the shorter one. A combination of polished aluminium and painted finish, producing handsome two-tone bodywork, was now offered as an optional extra to make the cars exceptionally attractive. The engine was reportedly tuned, the springs flattened, the steering raked, special shock absorbers fitted, the Morris braking left standard as it had already been improved, the handbrake placed on the right, instead of centrally, and a host of other detail changes made.

The third body option in the new range was the Super Sports Salonette,

'Old Number One' was the first Kimber product built specifically for sporting use, and arguably the first true MG

an all-aluminium closed body on the 8ft.6in. chassis. With two doors, an upright vee-shaped windscreen and a duck tail, these endearing machines didn't appear until early 1925, and were to number only six in total. All cars in this inviting new range had standard bullnose radiators and, tucked away below each door, a Morris Garages tread plate featuring no less than two MG octagons - the first time they had actually been applied to the cars. With inherently graceful and racy lines, reasonable performance and a £375 price tag, the Super Sports open tourers resembled scaled-down 3-litre Bentleys at a fraction of the cost. Plenty of favourable publicity was printed, and the Alfred Lane workshop was soon hectic once more.

Cecil Kimber's initiative and persistence had injected Morris Garages with a new lease of life. In March 1925 the small band of engineers finally completed 'Old Number One', though of course they didn't call it that then. The first Kimber product built specifically for sporting purposes, it was also the first Kimber vehicle to embody an almost completely new chassis owing little to Morris parentage. Putting performance way ahead of practicality, 'Old Number One' was a spartan, open sports car with a minimum of frills - in Kimber's eyes the first 'true' MG, the real ancestor of the rapid, positive sportsters for which the MG marque was to become famous. Registered on the 27th of that month, the car was later invariably described by confused P.R. men as the 'first MG'. Typically as ever, these chaps would also telescope the car's successful gold medal run (with Kimber at the wheel) in the 1925 London to Lands End trial with the MG founder's previous run two years before!

Based around a completely re-

Simple, spartan and efficient, 'Old Number One' was, in Cecil Kimber's eyes, most certainly the first true MG

engineered Morris Cowley chassis, 'Old Number One' was powered by an ohv 11.9hp Hotchkiss engine of 1547cc. Its construction involved a clever combination of standard and non-standard Morris components - for instance, the standard half-elliptic front springs, plus special half-elliptic rear springs in place of the usual Morris three-quarter-elliptic rear springs. With single plate clutch, orthodox three forward speed gearbox, Morris brakes and wire wheels, the car was rigid, efficient and fast in action. Kimber possibly had no time for sentimentality, for he sold his first 'true' MG soon after the Lands End run to a friend in Stockport, Cheshire. It then changed hands again, and was later spotted being used to haul a trailer loaded with pig food! Further deterioration found it in a Manchester scrapyard before being discovered by an MG employee and returned to the company in 1932. From that point on, it was hailed as 'Old Number One'. Though it was never called a Kimber 'special', that is what it truly was - a car inspired by Kimber, and built by those infected with his enormous enthusiasm; the forerunner of a great enthusiasts' marque.

A NEW BREED OF SPORTS CAR

Thanks to 'Old Number One', 1925 had already created a significant landmark in MG history. Of course, the car stayed with Cecil Kimber only briefly. He and his men were no doubt more concerned with a production line that was churning out extensively modified Morris Oxford chassis with MG bodywork supplied by outside contractors.

Based on what Morris Motors called the 14/28 Oxford chassis, the MG Super Sports model range quite naturally became known as 14/28 Super Sports MGs. Low, sporting, superbly finished, and breathtakingly attractive for their year, these cars created a healthy demand. Concerned, also, with producing various bodies on perfectly standard Morris Oxford chassis, the Morris Garages could not afford their staff much free time. Pleasurable as they found it, the small production staff were not carrying out their work in ideal conditions - unless construction of several cars per week within the Alfred Lane workshops' 2000sq.ft. can be termed ideal.

In September 1925, by courtesy of William Morris, MG car production moved into a portioned-off section of the Morris Motors radiator factory in Bainton Road, Oxford. Thus space, staff and production all increased. At the same time, the longer 9ft. wheelbase Morris chassis was standardised for both two seater and four seater MGs. Already the cars displayed some of the practical disadvantages of 'sports' cars. There were few complaints, however, about the increasingly used wire wheels, and the unashamedly rorty exhaust note that escaped from the 13.9hp, 1802cc side valve engines. Many detail changes, including minor tuning and thorough testing of each power unit, constantly improved the cars. With the general air of happiness that hung freely around the factory, an indefinable MG

23

atmosphere was already brewing. The men simply enjoyed their work.

Morris Garages products were now generally known as MGs, their growing individual identity betraying basic parentage only with the 'bullnose' radiators they always carried. But something of a shock was just around the corner. For the 1927 model year, the latest Morris Motors vehicles appeared in September 1926 with a more modern but less distinctive flat fronted radiator. A sweeping change, indeed, but not the only one. Morrises were now to use a wider, shorter wheelbase and heavier chassis frame as standard, leaving MGs with little option but to follow suit. Styled along similar lines to earlier cars, Kimber's forcibly redesigned range of open and closed bodies clothed cars that were not initially worthy successors to their early sisters. With approximately 400 'bullnose' MGs completed, the new models (rather indifferently dubbed 'flat-rads') benefited from their revised Morris chassis' improved handling, but suffered some visual deterioration and reduced performance. Their 14/28 Super Sports designation remained unaffected.

An inauspicious start for the 1927 model range it may have been, but very soon Cecil Kimber, Cecil Cousins and Morris engineer/MG enthusiast, Hubert Charles, were devising subtle improvements. Such was their devotion that a whole host of changes would eventually transform the new cars into appreciably better machines than their predecessors. Ride and handling benefited from flattened springs front and rear, and the use of Hartford rear shock absorbers. Braking was thoroughly redesigned, and the rubber-mounted steering replaced by an improved Marles assembly. Balloon, rather than beaded-edge tyres

were now standardised on all cars, a quieter exhaust system used, constructional changes made and the doors enlarged. Styling was improved by an engine-turned effect replacing the polished shine of the aluminium side body panels, and maintained by the retention of the established two-tone finish. A few pounds reduction saw the prices down to £340 for the open two seater, £350 for the open four seater, and £475 for the two or four seater Salonette fixed head. And very good value they were, too.

All these changes occupied most of the 1926/27 Winter. Despite much thumb-twiddling by patient enthusiasts on a production line awaiting a finalised design, once construction began the new range became an immediate hit with motorists. In only its first year of production, it equalled the total number of 'bullnose' MGs ever built. During that year the Octagon badge appeared on the radiator for the first time, initially fixed to the honeycomb and later placed with more belief at the radiator head. Whereas only their valve ports had been polished previously, the Morris engines were now further tuned with polished combustion chambers and stronger valve springs. A black stove-enamelled cylinder head proclaimed that the power unit was no longer simply a Morris 'lump'. Whatever the initial doubts about the latest MG Super Sports cars, they were snapped up by an eager public just as fast as the Bainton Road factory could create them.

The Morris Garages premises had been liberally sprinkled across Oxford since their earliest days. Now that Cecil Kimber's untiring enthusiasm had cleared the company so positively over its latest hurdle, the due reward was the need for yet larger premises to cope with ever increasing production.

The 14/40 four-seater tourer of the late twenties was one of the first MGs to feature a flat radiator

Naturally, Kimber sought the assistance of his boss William Morris, the man without whose financial support the MG identity would never have flourished. From his hard-fought beginnings and early struggles, W.R.M. had learnt the ways of necessary frugalities - he had always rolled his own cigarettes - but with little hesitation he agreed to finance the construction of a new factory for MG production. By Autumn 1927, the recently acquired Morris Garages depots at Merton Street (servicing), and Leopold Street (painting and repairs) were dwarfed by a new purpose-built MG factory in Edmund Road, Cowley, close to the Morris Motors establishment. Frugal or not, W.R.M. had forked out not much less than £20,000!

The new factory was once quoted by Kimber as being 'the only factory of its kind in the world devoted solely to the manufacture of sports cars'. Sure enough, the MG legend was growing fast. Potential weekly production was now up to thirty-five cars, only very few of which would represent Kimber's much loved excursions into special coachbuilders' versions of MGed Morris chassis. One of these was the 'Old Speckled Hen', an aptly named fabric covered saloon. It had even been known for coachbuilders to offer for public sale their own conversions of MGs - out-Kimbering Kimber, so to speak.

Due to the vagaries of historians, MGs of 1927 have been called both 14/28 models and 14/40 models. Whatever Kimber's reasons for allowing these questions to arise, one of these cars produced something of a surprise late in that year. Though hardly a racing car, it won a pukka motor race - at an average velocity of little less than 62 mph. Argentine was the country, the San Martin track near Buenos Aires the venue, and Alberto Sanchiz Cires the driver. It was MG's first track racing victory, another important milestone passed. Late 1927 also produced the first official designation of then current models as 14/40s, more precisely 14/40 Mk.IVs. Except in detail, these Super Sports models were unchanged. Needless to say, the attention lavished on their construction was as devoted as ever.

Strangely enough, 1928 brought with it a drop in demand for 14hp side valve MGs. Possibly the modest four cylinder engine was more susceptible to age in a sports car environment; maybe sporting motorists had expected a completely new model. Whatever the reason, 1928 production was to be 100 units down on the previous year's total. Even so, the year saw some important events take their place in the steady march forwards, not the least of which was the establishment in Spring of a new company called The M.G. Car Company (Proprietors: The Morris Garages Ltd.). Such things as the devising and publication of owners' handbooks, parts lists and service manuals were put into motion. Then, in June an octagonal instrument panel graced the dashboard for the very first time. Octagons suddenly sprouted elsewhere, too - the toe board, the accelerator pedal, the hub cap. Even the scuttle ventilators became octagonal. Then came a development of rather more significance.

For some years, the standard Morris chassis had been severely reorganised before being allowed to gain MG status. Engines, too, had been torn apart, tampered with to good effect, lovingly reassembled and thoroughly tested. 1928, however,

saw the attentions of MG engineers applied to William Morris' products with even greater enthusiasm. Running chassis were now subjected to all manner of rolling-road tests after being fitted with a multitude of MG-developed components. To describe these attentions as lavish is no exaggeration, yet still the MGs would often be called "rebodied Morrises". Certainly, it was somewhat illogical to tear so much off the Morris chassis, and at last MG arranged to buy bare chassis frames and engine/gearbox units from Morris Motors, and brake-endowed axles from Wolseley Motors Ltd., a company purchased by William Morris in 1927. This move logically led to MG designing and building their own chassis frame for the first time since 'Old Number One' - with highly impressive results.

The story began with the Morris Light Six that appeared at the 1927 Motor Show. This was a sort of stretched 9ft. 6in. wheelbase Morris Cowley powered by a new Morris 2468cc overhead-camshaft six-cylinder engine. Indeed, the whole machine had stretched a point too far, its chassis flexing enough to cause grave faults in its roadholding. While Morris, therefore, attempted to resolve matters by installing the same engine in an improved chassis, Cecil Kimber had snapped up a surviving Light Six in December 1927, wanting only the engine. A totally new chassis frame was now designed at the MG factory, and fabricated to incorporate a rebuilt Cowley rear axle, a new Alford and Adler front axle, half-elliptic springing front and rear, Marles steering and Morris/MG braking.

Only the second MG essay into chassis design, the finished product was displayed fully clothed on another of 1928's significant occasions, MG's first ever appearance at the Motor

An MG for the most affluent sporting motorist of the late twenties was the 18/80 Six with four-door Saloon de Luxe coachwork

Show. Known as the 18/80 MG Sports Six, the new car was an MG to suit the most discriminating buyer, to cater for the more affluent sporting motorist - the four seat tourer was £485, the two seat tourer £480, the two door Salonette £545 and the full four door saloon £555. Supplied as always by Carbodies of Coventry, the handsome bodywork was enhanced by racy centre-lock wire wheels. At its head was a brand new radiator style that would be a trademark for years hence. Once mounted, the driver was faced by an impressive array of instruments, with pedals and steering both fully adjustable. Delving into the Alvis, Lagonda market, this luxurious MG was actually quite reasonably priced.

Amongst the various body styles offered on the 18/80 Six was this four-seater open tourer

The 'Quick Six', as it soon became known, could thunder up to an exceptional 80mph, and hold the road to match. Its six cylinder Morris engine had naturally not escaped some sorting. A newly cast cylinder block added a second carburettor, and several major engine components were produced specially in polished aluminium. Its three speed gearbox only a mild handicap, the six cylinder engine featured an amazingly flexible torque curve - 8 to 80 mph was possible in top gear! Here was an MG in the Bentley tradition, right at the opposite end of the price and size scale to the second brand new MG that appeared on the Motor Show stand that active year.

The 18/80 MG Six Mk. 1 (to give it its full title) provided some of the impetus that launched MG into racing. Driven by Francis Samuelson, one example competed in the January 1920 Monte Carlo Rally, the first MG to do so. But it was the other new MG that shared the Motor Show stand with the Six (and the 14/40 Mk.IV) that was to stir up a whole new competitive spirit within the marque - the first MG Midget.

As already suggested, sporting motorists were probably eager to be wooed by a new breed of sports car.

With luck, maybe with judgement, the Midget broke this new ground at exactly the right moment. At the time, British cars were taxed in direct proportion to their R.A.C. formula horse-power. 1928's petrol tax further encouraged the use of small cars and, anyway, the baby Austin Seven had been enjoying a ready market since 1922. It was hardly surprising, therefore, that William Morris launched his rival 'baby', the 8hp 847cc powered Morris Minor in August 1928. This no doubt fired Cecil Kimber's imagination, the results of which had exactly the same effect on a great number of more economically minded sporting motorists.

An early prototype Morris Minor had somehow found its way into the Edmund Road factory. It was fitted with one of the Wolseley-designed four cylinder overhead camshaft engines that W.R.M. had thought too powerful and subsequently detuned for the Minor. Kimber had other views about the 20bhp unit's potential in an MG. Reliving early bullnose days, his operation on the Minor was simple and efficient. Off came the body to make

Announced late in 1928, the M-type Midget was the first MG to be produced in thousands rather than hundreds

way for a light two seater fabric-covered plywood shape on an ash frame. Limited chassis modifications involved lowering the suspension, and altering the pedal layout, gear change and steering rake. Standard Morris Minor wire wheels with MG hubcaps, a smaller version of the new standardised MG radiator, basic weather equipment, louvred side valances, a small vee-windscreen and cycle-type mudguards completed the attractive little sportster. It was soon to be dubbed 'the greatest sportscar in the world.'

Olympia show-goers must surely have been encouraged by the Midget's £175 price tag. Such was their interest that several hundred bodies were immediately ordered and a new assembly line laid down in the factory. The line did not grind into motion until April 1929 but, once started, it fairly whizzed along - the Midget was the first MG to be produced in thousands rather than hundreds. Much of this was due to the sudden growth of both motor sporting enthusiasm and participation. Whatever their mount and financial standing, streams of enthusiasts were taken with the idea of competition. Weighing 10cwt, the 20bhp Midget was there to capitalise.

The motoring magazines were filled with superlatives. *Autocar* in June 1930 said: "Sixty or sixty-five miles an hour are not adventure but delight - acceleration is very brisk - not unduly noisy - easy to manoeuvre - very steady even over poor surfaces - most excellent at hill-climbing - outwardly smart - altogether an extraordinarily fascinating little car." The *Motor* summed up similarly: "This exceptionally attractive little vehicle - one of the most fascinating we have ever driven." Allowing for the fact that journalists were rarely heavily critical in those days, it was still a joyous

introduction. Sports car history was in the making.

Cecil Kimber's motor sporting aspirations had at last been given a much needed chance to blossom. Following a satisfactory showing on the Easter 1929 Lands End Trial, an eye was cast towards Brooklands. A team of three Midgets, driven by the Earl of March, Callingham and Parker, was prepared for the Junior Car Club's High Speed Trial in June. Bolstered by two privately owned cars, the Midget phenomenon began in style that day, with all cars gaining gold medals in the course of setting the three fastest times of the day. From now on Kimber would display more and more interest in competition, a policy that would lead the MG marque to worldwide fame.

Yet another new car was to appear at Edmund Road before the end of 1929. It was a development of the 18/80 Six theme, a new version to complement rather than replace the old. The Mk. II featured a heavier and more rigid chassis, a wider track, a four-speed gear box, sturdier final drive and much improved cable operated brakes. The redesign was so thorough that the Mk. II was 3 cwt. heavier than the Mk. I, and about £100 dearer. Retaining the standard 2468cc six cylinder engine, it was thus slower, probably reason enough for its failure to sell as well as its predecessor. Both models would remain in production for some time yet, but would sell slowly enough to leave a residue of new vehicles in stock during the early thirties well after the production men had finished building them. It was the little Midget that hogged the sales return sheets and created the old problem once again of insufficient production capacity. Another move was necessary - to Abingdon-on-Thames.

The diminutive Midget stimulated some rapid growth in enthusiasm for motor sport

ABINGDON AND THE MIGHTY MIDGETS

The Great War of 1914-18 had kept the Pavlova Leather Company of Abingdon-on-Thames fully stretched making fleece-lined leather trench-coats for the troops. But in post war years the recession in demand for its goods had left the company's plant with space to spare, space to let. Despite the premises being far from ideal for automobile production, it was to here that the MG Car Company moved in the autumn of 1929. At least the old leather works provided room to move - conditions at the multi-thousand pound purpose-built Edmund Road factory had become totally overcrowded only two years after opening.

Spearheaded so typically by the founder, a long determined struggle had transported those early special bodied Morris MGs from a sometimes vague identity to becoming a strong, distinct and separate marque in their own right. And now there was a

factory with floor space of no less than 175,000sq.ft. to prove it. A sleepy but attractive settlement, Abingdon would never be the same again. Little could the locals have considered that their village was to become synonymous with sports car production. MG historian F. Wilson McComb later described Abingdon very aptly: 'That sleepy little Thames-side village where the cows leave octagonal hoof marks'.

If the Edmund Road factory had seemed expensive, the extent to which W.R. Morris' financial support was backing MG's arrival in Abingdon made the earlier outlay insignificant in comparison. For the marque's new home promised true mass production. This wouldn't mean any dilution of that ever growing phenomenon, the MG 'atmosphere'. To ensure that a tradition of craftsmanship was main-tained and that the MG spirit be reflec-ted in the cars, Kimber now gathered his followers around him. Most of the

31

The magnificent 'Tigress' was officially designated the 18/100 Mk.111. It was not a great success, and only five were built

old-timers stayed on, while several new members joined the team, among them Sydney Enever. The accent was on gifted talent rather than theoretical qualifications - thus the 'atmosphere' would grow. As the production lines were gradually organised at Abingdon, MG's selection of bodies on three separate chassis totalled many different versions. Base models were the 14/40 Mk.IV (soon to be discontinued), the 18/80 Sixes (Mk.I and Mk.II) and the new Midget, now generally referred to as the M-type Midget.

The M-type Midget was destined for the record books as the first MG ever to achieve four figure sales. But, for the moment, much of the MG workforce was preoccupied with another first, the first MG built specifically for racing. Known as the 18/80 Mk.III, it was based on the recently modified Mk.II chassis, with a developed 18/80 2468cc power unit featuring a crossflow cylinder head and dry sump lubrication amongst many other refinements. Hopes of an increase in power output to 100bhp led

to the designation 18/100 Mk.III, though even after studied effort that figure was never achieved. A much nicer title for the magnificent, imposing machine was the 'Tiger' (or more commonly, Tigress) as it came to be known. Into this car were built, almost regardless of cost, both the Bentley tradition and the earliest ambitions of the MG men for a true road racing model.

The race in which these earliest ambitions were to be given their head, and ultimately severely dented, was the May 1930 Brooklands Double Twelve 24-hour event. Handsomely bodied with cycle-type mudguards, four full seats and outside exhaust, the 18/100 Mk.III was, like its predecessor, rather over-weight. Whether this, or the engine's dislike of sustained high speed running, was the major factor in its demise is not clear but, either way, the Double Twelve was the car's first and last race under company jurisdiction. Callingham and Parker co-drove it for only two hours before engine failure that day. The Mk.III was not a sales success either. Available from the factory at £895 absolutely ready for (track) battle, it was perhaps a little behind its time in terms of size and value for money. Only five 'Tigresses' were ever built despite the wide ripple of interest that one example created at the 1930 Motor Show.

The Tigress's demise in the Double Twelve race was over-shadowed by a rather more significant result of that event. It concerned the amazing little M-type Midget. Since its announcement at the 1928 Motor Show and during subsequent produc-tion, the car had already gained a reputation for value, economical running and motor sporting suitability. Given detail improvements during its first production year, it had been raced with success worldwide. In short, the car which *Motor Sport* magazine had innocently described as: "A little gem of a car, fit to take two people and their luggage anywhere, happy as could be!", had already stated its claims to making sports car history. Cecil Kimber's competitive instincts had thus been energised and, as Abingdon already had something of a small racing department, attention was focussed on developing the Midget. By the time of the 1930 Brooklands Double Twelve, Reg Jackson and Hubert Charles had together squeezed 7bhp extra from the 847cc engine. For the race, five cars were built with these 27bhp, tuned engines, Brooklands exhaust systems, larger fuel tanks and slightly revised bodies with cut-away doors. The effort paid off. Although outpowered by many of their rivals, the five Midgets capably suffered those long hours at high speed over the bumpy track, and caused great delight at Abingdon by taking the Team Prize. Dubbed 'The Tomato Growers', the team proved s o m e w h a t m o r e t h a n m e r e agricultural ability that day!

Predictably enough, a Double Twelve Replica M-type variant was added (at £245) to the Midget range, which now also included the Midget Sportsman's Coupé, a delightful little machine that had been introduced sometime previously. Virtually a thirties-style Mini-Cooper, the Sportman's Coupé immediately made a great impact. Two particular Midget customers of this period are worthy of note. One was Edsel, son of Henry Ford, who imported a car into the USA early in 1930 with which to surprise his fashionable acquaintances. The other was a fellow named John Thorn-ley who bought his car soon after. Via that car, Thornley became a founder member of the MG Car Club, and even-tually general manager of the MG Car Company itself.

Late in 1930 Cecil Kimber adopted a memorable new sales slogan - "Safety Fast!". No doubt with this in mind, customers appeared in droves to buy the M-type Midget. Many detail developments were made during the model's production life and, after appearing in 1931 at the Motor Show for the fourth time, the M-type was eventually phased out in 1932. No less than 3235 examples had been built. Well before that, however, several new Midgets had appeared to further the model's reputation. During 1930 MG had built a prototype 6ft. 9 in. wheelbase chassis with its two main members swept up over the front axle, but passed below the rear axle. Designated EX. 120, this chassis was destined for the company's first attempt at international speed records.

Record breakers of some repute, Captain George Eyston and Ernest Eldridge were after the Class H (up to 750cc) speed record. Under Eldridge's direction, a special factory workshop now developed an almost completely new, but M-type 847cc-derived, 750cc engine for the EX.120. Fitted with a special pointed tail body, the first MG record car was ready by late 1930. Aiming for the magical first ever 100mph by a 750cc car, EX.120 fell somewhat short during its first attempt at Montlhéry track in France. But after some rushed development, which included the fitting of a supercharger, Eyston tried again only a short time later in February 1931. This time - success! Several records at over 100mph became the property of MG.

It is difficult to realise just how incredible that achievement was in 1931 when nowadays many road cars can achieve 150mph, a hallowed few almost 200mph. Even so, MG had made quite a landmark, and the follow-up was rapid. It was announced that the Montlhéry success had inspired a new 750cc racing Midget available to the racing man both with and without supercharger. Known as the Montlhéry, or C-type, Midget, the new racer was based on EX.120's 6ft. 9in. wheelbase ladder chassis with a redesigned 746cc version of the record breaker's power unit. Different in almost every detail, the engine was

The C-type Montlhéry Midget racer was inspired by MG's earliest international speed record attempts at Montlhéry race-track in France

only distantly related in its overhead camshaft layout. All springing was semi-elliptic, wheels were of centre-lock wire spoke design and the doorless aluminium bodies were of EX.120-derived, pointed-tail design, right down to the scuttle wing deflectors and cowled radiator.

In the 750cc class, 1931 was truly the Montlhéry Midget's year. Built in an organised rush, the first batch of cars made their debut at that year's Brooklands Double Twelve race. In an extraordinary result, no less than seven of them completed the distance (gaining the Team Prize), five of them taking the first five places! It was an incredible triumph at a time when Cecil Kimber had desperately wanted to follow up MG's 100mph record, despite a general depression in the motor industry which hadn't left his company untouched. But there was more to come. Amidst a host of 1931 victories too numerous to mention, the Montlhéry Midget gained outright victory and Team Prize at the Irish Grand Prix, and mere victory at the Ulster T.T., these being two of the most important British races of the day. Built to order, and mildly developed until mid-1932, this famous MG racer was assured of a place in motoring history - and with only 44 being com-

Available open or closed, but only in four-seater form, the attractive F1 Magna promised, somewhat misleadingly, the image of high performance

pleted, assured, too, of a healthy future demand from collectors.

At a time when the MG initials were becoming world famous in motor racing, the EX.120 record car met an untimely end with one final flourish. George Eyston had returned to Montlhéry to cover 100mph plus in one hour. He succeeded, all right, but with another record pocketed, Eyston left his driving seat rather sharply when the car burst into flames and recycled itself into a charred ruin. Luckily, a successor had already been constructed - EX.127, with engine of similar displacement, and its driver placed low in a new aerodynamic body. Called the 'Magic Midget', this record breaker had pushed the Class H speed record up to 114.77mph by the

end of 1931, and was to break the 120mph mark exactly one year later. Later still, in October 1936 at Frankfurt, the then ageing car was to make it 140.6mph.

While all this record breaking and racing was taking place, the MG Car Company had to earn a crust. Such valuable commercial prestige had, of course, been attained courtesy of the income from MG production car sales. It had also been achieved, it seemed, at the cost of 25% loss in production. As already noted, MGs had not completely escaped the attention of the automotive depression. It was no help that several of their production models were now rather elderly. Still available were the old 18/80 models and the two versions of the 1928 vintage M-type Midget. Late in 1931, two new models appeared without becoming overnight sensations. Both the new chassis were stretched versions of the Montlhéry C-type

This Midget J1 tourer was part of the new Midget range unveiled in 1932

Considered one of the classic sports cars of all time, the J2 Midget enjoyed a clever combination of performance and simplicity

Following the high performance J3 Midget came the out-and-out racing J4 – minus doors, of course

Midget unit. Of 7ft. wheelbase, one was the basis of the new F-type Magna. Also available with two body options, this car used a Wolseley Hornet-based 1271cc six cylinder ohc engine. Both new cars had plenty of things in common - half elliptic, sliding trunnion suspension, centre-lock wire wheels, axles, steering gear, 8in. drum brakes, modest performance and inability to set the MG sales return sheets alight. But the MG design team had a trump card up their sleeves.

For the 1932/33 model year, the key was unveiled in August 1932 in the form of the new Midget J-type range. Whereas the J1 was offered with four seater open or closed bodywork, the J2 was strictly a two seater, but all the more charming for it. Indeed, with cut-away doors, double-humped scuttle and cut-off tail, it was a masterpiece of race-bred, economical and functional design. In setting a truly dateless sportscar fashion, the J2 was soon to be considered by many as one of the classic sports cars of all time. The J1 merely looked nice! Both cars used a chassis following well-tried C-type Midget practice, and were powered by a race-developed version of the (originally Wolseley) M-type 847cc engine, brought back up from its 746cc C-type Midget days. With crossflow 8-port cylinder head and twin SU carburettors, this unit now produced 36bhp at 5500rpm, at the time an impressive rev figure. Naturally half-elliptic sprung, the chassis used the 7ft.2in. wheelbase that the D-type Midget had adopted later in its life.

Selling for just under £200 (the J1 cost somewhat more), the J2's clever simplicity made it an excellent proposition for the youngster. It wasn't without faults though. The expected 80mph could rarely be achieved, the crankshaft wasn't always too

enthusiastic about the engine's high revving ability, and the 8in. drum brakes quite often didn't! But over 2000 were produced, and the car was great fun in action. Late in 1932 that action could take in track as well as road use with the J3 and J4 performance and racing derivatives, the latter not actually in production until early the next year. Powered by a supercharged 746cc engine very similar to that of the earlier C-type, both J3 and J4 were fast - J3 just enough for those with mild sporting aspirations, the J4 fast enough to warrant a new 12in. drum braking system. Indeed, the J4 was quite a handful at speed, and very few drivers could exploit its full potential.

With the MG model range already very adequately varied, the 1932 Motor Show produced several more designations. The 1271cc engined Magna had become F2 designated, thanks to its 7ft.10in. chassis gaining 12in. diameter brakes and a stretched two-seat version of the pretty J2 Midget body. The four-seater Magna now became the F3 in either open or closed form. A totally new and far more important range of vehicles was also introduced with the first of the Magnette K-series, the K1 and K2. These vehicles used the now well established MG chassis layout, but of two wheelbases (9ft. and 7ft. 10 3/16in.), with more track and braked by 13in. drums. Although of a smaller 1087cc, the engine was an improved version of the Magna unit with crossflow head and stronger crankshaft. The longer wheelbase chassis was restricted to K1 designation with a very attractive, pillarless, four door, four seat closed body. By early 1933 this model was also available with open four seater bodywork. Using the shorter wheelbase chassis, the K2 was restric-

Shown as it first appeared, the Magnette K1 with handsome pillarless saloon bodywork

ted to two seats. Cutaway doors distinguished the open models, while sweeping front wings were fitted to both types.

As if the model range was not already confusing enough, by mid-1933 the Magnettes had used four different engines and five different bodies, all creating a bewildering selection of designations. Yet only very small quantities were produced of each one! Worse still, the L-series Magna appeared early in 1933 with an improved K-series 1087cc ohc engine pushing out 41bhp. This model used the long wheelbase K-series chassis, but with the earlier 3ft. 6in. track instead of the K-series 4ft. track. Known as L1s with four seater open or closed bodies and as L2s with two seater open bodies, these Magnas looked very similar to other MGs of their period.

Despite the ever confusing pieces of this Abingdon jigsaw puzzle, somewhat improved sales were effected. One K-series Magnette stood head and shoulders above the rest. Of course, it was a competition version - the K3. Further victory, another Team Prize and Class H record had already been grabbed by C-type Midgets at the 1932 Brooklands 500 miles race. But early in 1933 there appeared just about the most famous racing MG of

It is believed only 15 Magnette K2s were built, all in two-seater open form

The Magna L1 four-seater. Its L2 sister shared similar lines but had only two seats

all. The K3 was in essence a supercharged 1087cc two seater bodied K2. Rugged and well equipped, its chassis was of the K2's 7ft. 10 3/16in. wheelbase with half-elliptic front and rear springs. While a one-off K3 prototype was finding success by finishing the 1933 Monte Carlo Rally and even performing fastest time of the day on the Mont des Mules hillclimb, another prototype was being tested. The scene was Italy - more precisely the very route of the classic Mille Miglia, a unique and often frightening race fought out over 1000 miles of public roads from Brescia to Rome and back.

The 1933 Mille Miglia wasn't to mark MG's debut in this race. Lord de Clifford and T.V.G.Selby had piloted a supercharged Montlhéry Midget there the previous year. The business-like projectile had caused both great interest and consternation among race-crazy Italians - one newspaper had printed a report including, "MG - Molta Guancia, Molta Gloria" (much impudence, much glory). No doubt one and all had breathed a sigh of relief

The Magna L1 in four-seater salonette guise

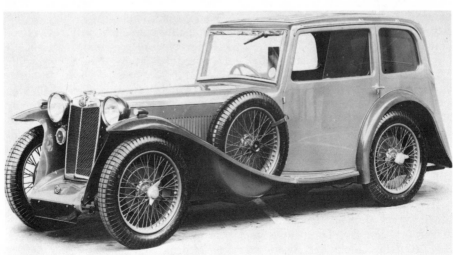

when the MG's camshaft drive sheared on the return to Brescia. But 1933's effort was to be more intensive. Lord Howe had been to see Sir William Morris personally about entering a team of three K3s at his own expense. Hence one of the prototypes reconnoitring the course so thoroughly, often in the hands of the legendary Count Johnny Lurani.

So serious was the Mille Miglia effort that the K3 was further developed with new steering gear and a stronger front axle in the short weeks of early 1933 before the race. Furthermore, the entire team operation was planned with great efficiency. On race day proper, three supercharged 1087cc K3 Magnettes sat on the grid after what had truly been a very short gestation period for a brand new car. Amongst the famous Italian racing drivers of the day, Lord Howe and Hugh Hamilton in one car, Eyston and

Lurani in the second and Birkin plus Bernard Rubin in the third all received a great welcome from the Italian crowds. A twinkle in their eyes had not divulged their well prepared plans. Off hared Birkin to pile enormous early pressure on the dangerously fast Maseratis. This ploy pushed the Italians too hard, too early, and effectively disposed of them - Birkin's K3 too, unfortunately, though only after he had broken many records. Anyway, the road ahead was now much clearer for the remaining MGs, indeed, clear enough for them to grab the first two places in their class, the Eyston/Lurani car also being first car over the line.

Quite possibly the Italians were bewildered by this daring MG coup, for the team even walked off with the team prize - the first time a non-Italian marque had done so. Quite certainly Sir William Morris was agreeably pleased on commenting: "The victory

The rugged Magnette K3 chassis was essentially the K2 unit with a supercharged 1087cc power unit. The K3 was to become one of the most famous racing MGs ever

of the MG Magnette in the Italian 1000 miles road race will go down in history as one of the finest achievements of a British light car. It was a venture fully in keeping with the best sporting traditions". Of course, that was what MGs were all about.

The marque had now set a pattern that would take them through the remainder of 1933 to a peak of racing achievements over the next two years. As for 1933, further notable results were gained at Le Mans, the Nürburgring (where Hamilton's full race J4 Midget won its class, but was rather overshadowed by K3 fever elsewhere), Brooklands and again in Italy on the Coppa Acerbo event. Perhaps the most memorable occasion was when the great Italian ace, Nuvolari, was persuaded by Lord Howe to drive a K3 in the Ulster T.T. In glorious style, Nuvolari smashed the class lap record several times during

an epic race-long battle with Hamilton's J4, and was first across the finish line at a record speed that wasn't to be bettered until Stirling Moss' efforts in 1951.

MG racing cars were now in great demand. All over the world those initials were prominent on result sheets. Though substantial, the company's investment in its racing activities was not ruinous and had given the name an enviable ring. But if MG racing success was to continue, a continuous pattern of development had to be maintained simply to keep up with the racers' mischievous ability to date rather rapidly. Likewise, road car sales needed constant prodding. And to compound matters, Sir William Morris had kept a beady eye on the MG situation. Despite his pleasure over the Mille Miglia victory, his heart never beat with the stimulation of racing's lusty roar.

41

This special-bodied Magnette K3 was built by Jensen

PROLIFIC PRODUCTION IN THE THIRTIES

Like so many other thirties' motor car manufacturers MG were marketing a bewildering range of models that effectively was far too diverse. By early 1934 several models, including the J-type Midgets, the L-type Magnas and the K-type Magnettes had all been discontinued. The loudest cries of anguish were probably over the great little J2's dismissal. This delectable sportster had really warmed the blood of sports car enthusiasts. But its engine needed improvements that were for-

Taking over where the much loved J2 Midget left off came the very improved P-type Midget, this one is in two-seater form

This is the four-seater version of the PA Midget

bidden by the already overburdened two-bearing crankshaft. Continuing MG's policy of an incessant flow of new models, the P-series Midget was ready for its bow. It was March 1934 when the curtain was raised.

The P-type Midget harked back to its earlier sisters all right, but was fashioned as a much tougher car all round. Its new 847cc four-cylinder engine had an altogether heavier and stronger crankshaft with three main bearings. Producing 35bhp at 5600rpm (fractionally less than the J2 engine's output), the new power unit made up for any power loss with greatly increased durability and much smoother running. Retaining the J2's 3ft. 6in. track, the P's chassis was of a wheelbase about 1.25 in. longer, and of stronger construction. Other improvements included a better clutch and gearbox, and larger 12in. drum brakes. Typically Midget-styled, the P-type body, offered in two and four-seat open form, was actually roomier and better appointed. It seemed hardly likely that the old 'MG rheumatic elbow' complaint would be banished for ever, but most enthusiasts would now be much happier in the warmer, drier and more comfortable cockpit. £220 would buy the two seater, £240

the four seater. With sweeping wings and cut-away doors, the P-type Midget was well styled and attractive. Even prettier was the specialist coachbuilt Airline Coupé version available soon after the car's introduction.

Owing much to experience gained with the Magnas and Magnettes, the P-type was an excellent car with which to continue the Midget tradition. Unfortunately, it was a little overweight, and therefore represented no advances in performance. To the already growing division of diehard MG enthusiasts, this was indeed a retrograde step, and thus was established another MG tradition that was to be honoured (not always without reason) thereafter – to heap abuse on each new model the moment it appeared!

As the first P-type Midget, this car was subsequently known as the PA. Despite initial diehard reaction, the car was well received by the public, and about 2000 were constructed. The diehards soon learned that the stronger power unit responded well to tuning and, with many superchargers available for it, MG even undertook to continue their guarantee provided the recommended unit was fitted.

Only weeks after the P-type's birth came that of another new range – the Magnettes, now much improved into N-type designation. Again the

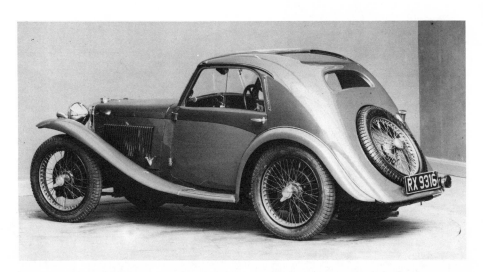

The very pretty Airline Coupé was based on the P-type Midget

result of studied improvement and much beefing-up, the N-type was powered by a developed and more powerful version of the 1271cc engine that was used in some of the K-type Magnette variants. Output was 56bhp, a healthy figure to bundle along a mature MG, available in two or four-seater open form plus, of course, specialist coachwork versions, one of which was the Airline Coupé. The factory-built cars had open bodies somewhat tall at the waist, but a two-tone colour scheme did much to reduce this effect. Interestingly, the fuel tank was now concealed within a shapely tail. Both P-type and N-type were to be gradually improved with developed versions over the next year.

With the MG model range reorganising itself, racing naturally continued in abundance. Straight into action came a P-type driven by Les Murphy to victory in the Australian Grand Prix of 1934, while another example finished at Le Mans soon after. At the Whit Monday Brooklands meeting that year, a brand new racing Midget gained a brand new 750cc lap

A very mature Magnette – the four-seater NA tourer

45

Above: On a driving test at Beaulieu in 1977. This Cresta-bodied NA Magnette is one of only twelve built by the coachbuilders Bertelli
Below: With a supercharged 746cc engine, the uncompromising Q-type Midget was so fiery that few drivers could cope with it. Only eight were built

record. It was the (to be short-lived) Q-type Midget, a combination of K3 and N-type components that looked very similar to the later pointed-tail 1934 versions of the K3. One particular detail was quite new, however. This was the Q-type's high pressure Zoller supercharger that pushed the engine's output up to well over 100bhp. Later, in fully developed form, this figure was to rise to an incredible 146bhp! All that from an old engine that in original 847cc form had pushed out only 20bhp.

So shatteringly quick were the Q-types that few drivers could handle them, and only eight were ever built. However, this did not deter one of them from later grabbing for all time the Brooklands Outer Circuit class H record at a fastish 122.4mph. Mention has already been made of the P-type Midget's racing debut as part of MG's 1934 onslaught. Successes were as common as ever that year, but not all was roses. Following its 1933 Mille Miglia triumph, the K3 Magnette now returned to the scene for a second attempt. Of the trio entered, however, only the Lurani/Penn-Hughes car finished the race – but well and truly behind the winner, about 1.5 hours behind him in fact! More in keeping with the MG reputation was the result of the Isle of Man's Mannin Beg race

that year – from nineteen starters only eight cars finished, no less than seven of them MGs!

Other memorable results that year came at Le Mans, at Brooklands (the British Empire Trophy), in Italy, Switzerland and France. Captain George Eyston was still breaking records too, but now in Class G in his K3-based EX.135 prototype. 128.69mph over the mile and 120.88mph in the hour were his two latest. Painted dramatically in cream and brown stripes, EX.135 was soon known as 'the Humbug'! For the year's most important British sports car event, the Ulster T.T., supercharged cars were to be excluded. This led to some rapid development on the N-type Magnette to boost its power output from 56bhp at 5700rpm to 74bhp at 6500rpm. Called the NE, the racer gained a remarkable victory in the T.T. despite severe handicapping in favour of the larger cars. Nevertheless, it was the only car to finish out of six entered that day, and perhaps this was a warning of things to come – the E.R.A. racing car for one.

Startlingly decked out in brown and cream stripes, Captain George Eyston's EX.135 prototype soon became known as 'The Humbug'. It quickly had many international records thoroughly beaten

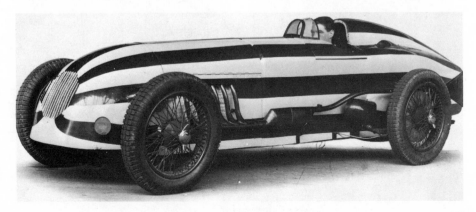

Above: Last of the K-type Magnettes was the KN, a combination of an N-type engine and K1 chassis

Below: Very similar to its predecessor, the NA, the NB Magnette enjoyed a lower scuttle line and a more pleasing appearance

On the production car side, the aforementioned improvements to the N-type Magnette had been under way. In the autumn of 1934 there appeared the KN. This vehicle was a combination of the latest 1271cc 56bhp N-type power unit with the great many remaining Magnette K1 9ft. long wheelbase chassis clothed with attractive four-seater pillarless saloon bodies, albeit by now facelifted. The combination sold far better than the original 38bhp K1s had done. Another special concoction was the ND, a standard N-type 8ft. wheelbase, 1271cc engined chassis fitted with what was left of the K2 open two seater bodies. Into 1935 the standard N-type became the developed NB with detail mechanical changes, and bodywork restyled to lower the awkwardly high waistline. This model was to carry on quite successfully into 1936.

Sold in double and treble figures, these specialised MG production varieties nevertheless were unimportant compared with the only ten examples of a new racer built in 1935. Known as the R-type Midget, the car was revolutionary in two ways – one, it was the first and only genuine single seat racer ever to be offered by MG to the public; two, it was the subject of an investigation into independent suspension design by chief designer Hubert Charles. The problems with the Q-type racer had been its hard suspension (and therefore bump reaction tendency) and its inability to put all its power to the ground (the huge power output caused severe wheelspin). It was thus felt that independent suspension might be the answer. But, in view of the project's ambitious nature and the limitations imposed on the design team, severe economies had to be made in the car's construction.

Announced in April 1935, the R-type featured a stiff, Y-shaped backbone chassis with hastily concocted wishbone and torsion bar independent suspension. The power unit was basically the Q-type's Zoller supercharged 746cc unit, but with several detail changes, principally to the induction system. Diminutive and narrow, the *monoposto* body caused mixed feelings, though certainly looked the part of a miniature Grand Prix car. Indeed, available to any motor racing enthusiast with a mere £750 to spare, the car caused something of a deserved fuss.

The fact that an R-type immediately won its class first time out in the International Trophy at Brooklands during May 1935 failed to cloud the car's lack of development. One problem was that 'Safety Fast' wasn't necessarily a term that drivers readily applied to their R-types. In fact, the independent suspension geometry allowed the body to roll so much on corners that the sensation was at first unfamiliar, unpleasant and frightening! Following the Brooklands outing, an 1100cc class win in the French Grand Prix was amongst several notable results gained by the R-type. But, with an improved Mk.2 version planned, something else was in the air. And this 'something else' was just possibly partly due to both the R-type's appearance and its suggested development. If this first true single-seat MG racer was a classic (as suggested), it was indeed ironic that it might have caused an imminent and staggering statement ... .

In 1934 Sir William Morris had become Lord Nuffield. As has been made clear throughout this MG history, Morris never really warmed to the thrill of motor racing. Indeed, as owner of The MG Car Company Ltd., he just about tolerated it. But over 1934 and 1935 the whole vast Nuffield empire underwent a great business and financial reorganisation. A forthright Yorkshireman named Leonard Lord was appointed to clear out the cobwebs, and it was he who became the new managing director of The MG Car Company Ltd. when Nuffield, without emotion, sold the famous racebred company to Morris Motors Ltd. in July 1935. Virtually overnight it was decreed that all MG works-involved racing activities should cease immediately. Though Cecil Kimber was later to regain company control upon Lord's resignation, things would never again be the same at Abingdon.

There was no way that Abingdon could be its real self without its design, experimental and racing departments, and sadly these all disappeared with the Morris Motors takeover. But equally draining to the great name was in fact that many of the enthusiastic staff departed and, of course, Kimber was no longer the MG figurehead for everyone to respect. That position now theoretically belonged to Leonard Lord. He was unquestionably a commercially minded and hard-headed businessman, not the sort of man with the emotion or desire to make heartfelt

The PB Midget was essentially a larger-engined PA, and a much better car into the bargain

decisions. Many a motoring enthusiast the world over was absolutely horrified at this sudden wind of change sweeping through MG.

If emotion were held aside, there was a grain of sense in a takeover that made one of the world leaders in sports car design part of a huge, unwieldy organisation. It was that MG models could incorporate many more off-the-shelf Nuffield components. Thus they could stay in production longer, present easier simpler serviceability and hopefully reverse the still steadily falling MG annual sales graph. Following the takeover, several model changes were made for the 1935/36 model year. Known as the PA, the first P-type Midget had represented many improvements over the much loved J2, but had not performed in expected fashion. Late in 1935, therefore, the P-type 847cc engine's cylinder bore was increased to 60mm (from 57mm), producing a 939cc capacity and uprating power from 35 to 43bhp. This certainly had the desired effect, and the PB, as it was known, was a far more desirable car than its predecessor. Even so, little over a quarter as many were produced before the model's end in mid-1936.

During 1934 and 1935 three P-series Midgets had earned themselves quite a reputation for their perfor-

mances in trials events, a relatively inexpensive sport for the standard tune everyday car – as long as car and driver didn't mind getting covered in mud. As a team, the three cars were known as the 'Cream Crackers', a nickname applied because of their immaculate (at least, before events!) cream and brown paintwork. Particularly fast with superchargers fitted, three PBs took over the 'Cream Cracker' team places for 1936, their subsequent success attracting great attention. Another notable trials team were the 'Three Musketeers'. Indeed, between them, the two virtually swept the board that year.

The PB Midget was shown at the 1935 Motor Show. Another revised MG model present was the latest N-type Magnette, but causing much more of a fuss was the brand new SA model aimed at the larger car market. This designation could quite possibly have been applied to the single seat R-type racer's intended successor, but Lord Nuffield's far-reaching policy change now saw it applied to something very, very different. The SA was a large, graceful saloon, a prestige car introducing a whole new breed of MGs that would help modify the company image. Unfortunately, insurance companies had already stated their disapproval of stark, lively sports cars by imposing high premiums. No doubt this fact did not go unnoticed as the Nuffield empire poured their resources into the new and handsomely appointed carriage.

As was becoming their habit, the supposedly genuine MG enthusiasts refused to recognise the new offering as a genuine MG. Of course by Abingdon standards it wasn't – not forgetting that several of the earlier Magnettes weren't exactly small cars. But of a 10ft. 3in. wheelbase and 4ft.5in. track, the SA was the largest MG yet. The diehards' disgust was based on several points – the heavy, box-section Wolseley-based chassis being conventional to the core, the Lockheed hydraulically operated braking system, the bolt-on wheels, the synchromesh gearbox, the Wolseley Super Six-based 2 litre engine with pushrod operated valves and so on .... But of excellent overall balance, well trained road manners, sustained high performance capability (though ponderous acceleration) and true quality, the new MG was real value for money at only £375 with a beautifully proportioned saloon body. Other coachwork, a four-seat tourer and a handsome Tickford Coupé, came later.

Once in production the SA became known as the 2 litre – odd really, because before production commenced its engine had been enlarged to 2288cc. This wasn't the only change for production. Wheels became centre-lock and the gearbox became non-synchromesh. Once the line had begun churning cars out, however, detail and more radical changes became regular. This only emphasised the inefficiency of the now huge organisation running the MG company, and possibly suggested that the car had been of faulty design in the first place. Undoubtedly, though, the MG 2 litre was a handsome, elegant and refined conveyance. Eventually phased out on the outbreak of war in 1939, 2738 were built altogether.

It was only the purists that the 2 litre displeased, for a much wider public was reached by this MG. A car that created far more widespread disappointment was the VA (or 1 1/2 litre as it came to be known), a model introduced midway through 1937 as both a replacement for the N-type Magnettes and as a sort of scaled-down SA. This new middle-sized MG was, just like its bigger sister, based on

a sturdy, very conventional chassis. Of 1548cc and pushrod ohv type, the VA's engine pushed out 54bhp at 4500rpm, not really enough to propel the heavy car along at anything remotely resembling MG's breed of sporting performance. Considering that the open four-seat touring version tipped the scales at just over 22cwt, this wasn't surprising! Even so, it progressed smoothly and quietly, and was a relaxing car to drive. It followed its predecessor in featuring many detail changes over a production life eventually halted by war at a time when its numbers topped the 2000 mark with ease.

It was the VA's engine, albeit a tuned version, that during 1938 trials enthusiasts were to find very desirable as a transplant into their competition

The elegant SA saloon was the first all-new model to be introduced after MG had been amalgamated with Morris Motors in July 1935. It was also the largest MG to date

Midgets. But for the birth of these cars we must return to midway through 1936, when a whole new breed of Midgets had been announced. As ever the purists grunted and howled. In line with the other new era models, the T-series Midgets had pushrod ohv engines. They were certainly excellent cars, but there was no denying that a great change had swept over Abingdon. Cecil Kimber, customers and trade dealers had all found life very different under the Nuffield thumb. The MG company's whole atmosphere had been diluted – even muddled and confused. Thank heavens, then, that many private MG racing drivers still knew which direction to point their energies in. And continued to do so very successfully.

A combination of lower power output and undue bulk gave the VA quite a struggle to maintain MG-type sporting performance

PRE-WAR AND POST-WAR UPHEAVAL

Under Nuffield rule MG Abingdon could never be quite the same again. With terms dictated by economists and accountants, MG's more business-like approach was, however, going to see them operating far more profitably in the future. Though they would never again be at the head of the sports car design field, there was no denying that with the large SA and VA pushrod ohv models the company were moving into a much wider market. In producing these big, well-equipped touring cars, they were also remembering the pre-Midget MG image. But real sports cars had not been forgotten.

The PA and PB Midgets were often regarded as the best looking, best all-round MGs of the thirties. Progress, nevertheless, insisted on marching onwards. Midway through 1936 came the usual cries from the purists – the T-series Midgets had been announced, the TA starting the ball rolling. What the purists resented were, of course,

the usual signs of progress – the pushrod ohv engine derived from that of the recently introduced Morris Ten, the more comfortable, much roomier two place body and its accompanying luggage carrying facilities, the synchromesh gearbox and the hydraulic brakes. No doubt they did not resent the TA's price which, at £222 represented excellent value for money.

The new Midget's engine produced 52bhp at 5000rpm from 1292cc. By today's standards, 0-60mph in a whole 23 seconds sounds laughable for a sports car, but in 1936 it was a satisfactory MG performance. Maximum speed was about 77mph. Of 7ft.10in. wheelbase and 3ft.9in. track, the TA's chassis, at least, was of traditional MG layout, differing only with its boxed-in front section aiming for high rigidity. Options against the open two-seater body were the Airline Coupé and Tickford cóupe versions. It

55

First of the T-type Midgets was the TA of 1936, and not unnaturally it showed many Nuffield influences. MG purists were not pleased!

was, perhaps, two factors that signalled the TA as father of a new breed – the much improved ride qualities, and the ohv engine's practicality in keeping its tune without requiring anything like the attention the previous ohc units had demanded (proper maintenance of these had always needed a high level of mechanical skill). Adversely, though, the engine did not respond to further performance tuning. This didn't seem to affect the TA's mud sploshing ability.

During 1937 both the 'Cream Crackers' and the 'Three Musketeers' trials teams were TA-mounted, the former's cars painted cream and brown, the latter's red. There had already been growing unrest amongst

The attractive Tickford Coupé was an optional body on the TA Midget

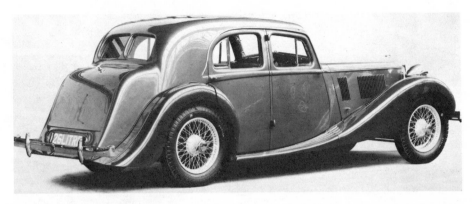

No doubt encouraged by the success of the SA and VA saloons, Abingdon produced the largest ever MG in 1938, the 2.6 litre WA

private entries at the resounding success of the factory sponsored trials cars. Not surprisingly, either, for having already dominated the scene during 1935 and 1936, the MG teams continued to do so in 1937 and 1938.

While the T-series Midgets were already giving an indication of their fame-to-be, MG's middle-size and large-size VA and SA carriages were stimulating MG sales, and thus the production lines. If the diehards had thought of these cars as ponderous, lumbering tractors, what must they have thought of August 1938's new outsize offering, the WA? Despite its wheelbase and front track being identical to that of the SA, and its rear

track only 3 inches wider at 4ft.8.75 in., the WA was in general terms certainly the largest production MG ever built. It was also the plushest. The emphasis throughout was again on refined performance with comfort. Based around the SA power unit, the WA engine had been taken out to 2561cc and the power increased to 95bhp at 4400rpm.

In action, the WA (also known as the 2.6 litre) trundled along in much the same way as its SA and VA sisters – with moderate acceleration and smooth, effortless and high cruising speeds. Thanks to its wider rear track it had improved rear seat comfort, and

Appearing just before the outbreak of war, the short-lived TB Midget was externally almost identical to the TA, but used the new Morris-derived XPAG engine

A typical Abingdon scene in the late
thirties, with purposeful no-frills sports
cars being built alongside luxury saloons

both saloon and coachbuilt coupé versions were available. With a certain ease these cars continued to raise the MG image, but by now war, in Europe at least, looked a fair probability. One more MG model was just going to have time to slip in before battle broke out.

For 1939 Morris Motors Ltd. designed for their Morris Ten a new 1292cc engine. Little did they realise that this power unit was to form the basis of the famous, record-bred XPAG unit upon which MG fortunes would rely for many years hence. More immediately, though, the engine was the one chosen to power the new MG Midget, the TB, available from mid-1939. Much modified by the MG engineers, the four cylinder engine's displacement dropped to 1250cc though it still managed to brew up 54bhp at 5200rpm. This was enough to propel the car along at constant high cruising speeds with a maximum around the 80mph mark. Most significantly, in MG form the new engine featured great reliability and extensive tuning opportunities – the latter not a feature enjoyed by the TA's power supply.

Although the mid and late thirties had seen MG factory support directed at the less demanding trials events, a great many privateers had continued to exploit their MGs in many forms of motor sport. Record breaking had perhaps brought the most notable results. As has already been mentioned, the old Magic Midget (EX.127) with 750cc engine reached 140.6mph in October 1936 at Frankfurt. One of the almost unnoticed names in the list of drivers who contributed towards the memorable MG clean-up in the Brooklands Double Twelve race back in 1931 had been that of a certain A.T.G.Gardner. By 1937 Gardner had not only become renowned as Major 'Goldie' Gardner but had also written

himself into several pages of the MG record books. For 1938, Cecil Kimber and Goldie Gardner put their heads together. With the Nuffield Organisation's approval they re-acquired Captain George Eyston's EX.135 Magic Magnette Class G record breaker which had been sold off during MG's reorganisation by Nuffield. The object was the achievement of yet more 1100cc Class G records.

With Lord Nuffield's knowledge, and surprisingly enough, his consent, EX.135 was rebuilt at Abingdon with an extremely sleek and low body to the design of Reid Railton. To decrease overall height, the driver was placed far lower than in a standard MG sports car. Indeed, only his head could be seen above the scuttle. Its engine supercharged by a Centric blower, EX.135 fairly rocketed through the records in November 1938. On a stretch of German autobahn near Frankfurt, Goldie Gardner was at the controls for a flying mile at an incredible 187.6mph, no less than 40mph quicker than Bobbie Kohlrausch's effort in 1936. Not content with that, Goldie Gardner easily raised the record the following year to a staggering 203.5mph for the flying kilometre – a memorable achievement.

Since MG had become part of Morris Motors in 1935, life for all MG-minded people had been rather different. Although the glamour had gone from Abingdon, the big luxury MGs had contributed quite some style to the MG image. Following a similar pattern were the competition exploits – although the racing axe had fallen, trials participation had been intense and record breaking had continued. Cecil Kimber, likewise, had departed from and been re-instated in his position as managing director. His control might thus have been irreparably eroded, but at least the new T-series

Quite possibly a forerunner of the
modern enclosed GT car, this sleek
mobile machine gun (hence the initials
on the body) was never offered to the
general public

Midgets were proving accomplished upholders of the MG tradition. What a shame it was that the outbreak of World War II in September 1939 should end all this. And end it at a time when a whole 3003 TAs had been built to overshadow the mere 379 TBs completed.

On the commencement of hostilities, MG's Abingdon factory discontinued car production immediately. War contracts were top priority in all factories during those uncertain times. Very soon, overhauled tanks, reconditioned machine guns, army trucks and light pressings for aircraft were leaving the factory instead of SAs, VAs, WAs, TAs and TBs. Then, in 1941, Cecil Kimber secured an important contract to make a section of the Albemarle aircraft, Britain's first nosewheel bomber. Unfortunately, he did so without prior consent of the Nuffield Organisation's board. This seemed a small oversight, but the action was to have a far-reaching and sad effect. The Nuffield group were already in discussion with the War Cabinet over armament contracts, and

deemed it necessary to have their whole operation spearheaded by one central control at Cowley. Cecil Kimber had done something somewhat contrary to Nuffield plans, therefore. The outcome was his sudden dismissal.

What a sad climax to an incredible career with MG. Yet, due to the country's and no doubt most of its motoring enthusiasts' preoccupation with the hubbub of war effort, the parting went almost without notice. While the Abingdon factory successfully continued its aircraft, tank and component work under the general management of long-time MG man George Propert, many industrialists bid for Kimber's talented services. Accordingly, in 1942 he joined Charlesworth, formerly coachbuilders and suppliers of many MG bodies, but now producing aircraft. From reorganising the Charlesworth factory, he moved on to doing the same job at the Specialoid Piston Company, setting a pattern of systems that would be utilised in many areas of the engineering industry.

During these war years Kimber did no more than consider a return to involvement with sports cars. Despite his love for them, his variable health might well have had a part to play in his eventual decision to stay clear of the motor car business, and concentrate on his great hobby of yachting. But he wasn't to get the chance ...

In view of Kimber's 'Safety Fast' slogan, and consequent excellent driving record, it was totally ironic that he should lose his life in a railway accident, more still that it should be something of a freak accident. But it happened. On the 4th February 1945 Kimber sat in the last coach of the 6pm

Returning to post-war production, Abingdon's first effort was the TC Midget

Peterborough train as it moved slowly out of King's Cross station. In clouds of smoke and steam, the train's powerful locomotive struggled, as all did, up the incline through the King's Cross tunnel. What most didn't do, however, was to grind to a standstill and start slipping back down the tunnel towards the station, but then the 6pm hadn't been afforded the rather necessary luxury of a second, assisting locomotive. The upshot of it was that, on seeing the train re-emerge backwards, the signalman pulled the points to divert it to another platform, but did so fractionally too late, causing the already-passing last coach to overturn. Such was Cecil Kimber's luck that he was thus killed in the crushed coach of a train rolling backwards at walking pace.

Without Kimber's leadership and guidance, MG cars would never have attained the respect and reputation that had been established before that ridiculous railway accident. Yet, devoid of their almost legendary

figurehead, the company was to enter a post-War era marked, thanks to their name, with ever greater worldwide acceptance.

Minus their guiding hand and now just part of a very large organisation, the MG Car Company nevertheless returned after the war to car production with some joy. That joy was not dampened by the unusual situation the country was in. The war had caused a terrible drain on resources. Quite naturally, raw materials were in great demand and were supplied to car manufacturers in relation to their product's export potential. New model development was right out of the question, particularly for a small cog which the big wheel was not going to look upon kindly as regards capital investment. Nevertheless, Abingdon was happy to clear out the various MG models of pre-war days, and concentrate on a slight development of a pre-war design as their only model. Thus the TB Midget evolved into the TC.

Production of the TC began late in 1945. Needless to say, the basic design was already well out of date, but a speedy return to volume production

Detail differences such as extra width did little to offset the TC's obvious resemblance to its pre-war sisters

and a rapid meeting of the great post-War demand for the new cars were the only considerations. In essence, the open two seater TC was little more than a slightly revised TB with a body much the same save for its 4in. extra width. Detail changes included the rear leaf springs slung by shackles instead of sliding trunnions, and minor modifications to the twin carburettor XPAG Morris Ten based 1250cc engine which did not change the output of 54bhp at 5200rpm. If in all other respects the car was still a TB, this did not have one iota's effect on the TC's immediate success. As the Government had intended, the first post-war MG quickly made inroads to export markets, not only in the various small demand countries of pre-War days, but most particularly in the British Commonwealth and North America.

Performance-wise, the TC was not dramatic at 20 seconds plus to 60mph and a maximum of around 77mph. However, the sheer joy and simplicity of driving such a nimble

Basic, simple and aimed at export, the TC surprisingly enough caught on in a big way in the one country where comfort was thought to be imperative, the USA

machine was about to catch on like an epidemic in the USA, where such a thing was perhaps most surprising of all. Americans, above all, like plenty of concessions to creature comforts in their cars, and the spartan little TC had virtually none, least of all such trappings as heaters, bumpers, soft springing and automatic transmission. But the gay, wind-in-the-hair sensation must have been intoxicating in the sports car desert that was America in those days. Not only that, but the TC was light on petrol, handled beautifully and was able to introduce sports car-racing for the first time to enthusiasts of modest means. In short, the TC introduced America to the sports car.

MG's latest success was soon

being used on race tracks all over the world. This would happen for many years thereafter, in the sixties and seventies, thanks largely to the strongly established (with branches worldwide) MG Car Club. Even in late 1949, with the TC model in its last days, Abingdon produced a tuning manual to encourage the 1250cc engine's wide tuneability. Such notables as Prince Philip, Clark Cable and racing driver Phil Hill all owned TCs during their early motoring days, Hill winning about a dozen races in his car whilst learning much of his skill. Demand was such that during the difficult 1947/48 period in Britain when petrol was virtually unobtainable, MG happily sold abroad almost as many cars as they could make and, in doing so, sowed the seeds of the company's wide-reaching, under-the-surface character change. No less than 10,000 TCs were built before the end of 1949, 6592 of them for export.

Whilst the Abingdon factory was

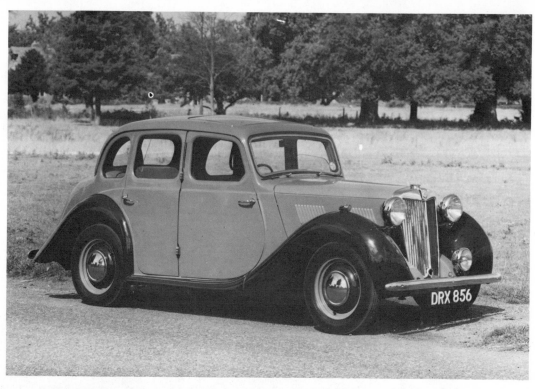

Above: First post-war MG saloon was the YA. In fact, it had been designed before the war

Below: Appropriately for the period, the Y-type was down-to-earth and conventional without sacrificing its high standards of comfort and road behaviour

having its work cut out in keeping up with the huge demand for the TC Midgets, it was only logical that a little time should be found for the old tradition – record breaking. But that was all it was, for there was no longer a Cecil Kimber to influence the Nuffield directors, and thus the competition restrictions were more thoroughly imposed than ever. With only occasional factory assistance, Goldie Gardner was now more or less out on his own. Undeterred, he had already resolved to

attack the still-standing 1936 Class H record of 140.6mph using a 741cc engine that had been designed by the factory before the war for just such a purpose, though never used. And so it was that as early as October 1946, with TC production accelerating by the month, Gardner piloted the re-engined EX.135 at 159.1mph over the flying mile on a public highway at Jebbeke, Belgium. What a partnership car and driver were proving to be!

Record breaking in 1947 saw

Seen here with a TC, the Y-type, too, was built in tourer guise with fold-down windscreen, though for export only

EX.135 managing only 118mph, but then the car only had 500ccs under its bonnet. Indeed, the power unit was an adjusted version of the previous year's 741cc engine, created for records in yet another class. 1947 was also the year of the new Y-series – a return to what promised to be an increasingly lucrative saloon market, more precisely the compact saloon market which MG had tapped so successfully with the 2400 1 1/2 litre VAs produced before the war. The Y-series had, in fact, been designed before the war, but didn't eventually reach production until early 1947. Like the VA, it was a product of the Nuffield Organisation but had none of the same style, preferring to achieve its reputation in down-to-earth, conventional fashion. In post-war times this was obviously highly appropriate, for the Y-series was to become the most successful MG saloon to date.

Although powered by a single carburettor version of the TC's 1250

With 10,000 examples produced in four years and over half of them going for export, the TC Midget introduced America to the sports car, and Abingdon to mass production

engine, the Y-type's chassis differed considerably from that of its sports car counterpart. Of 8ft.3in. wheelbase, 3ft.11 3/8in. front track and 4ft.2in. rear track, it was a box section frame underslung at the rear, where suspension was by semi-elliptic leaf springs. At the other end were independent units by coil springs and wishbones, the first such application to a Nuffield production car. Steering was also an MG first – by rack and pinion. Bodied with a four door saloon assembly very closely derived from those of the Morris and Wolseley 8s, the Y-type was luxuriously furnished, although of compact dimensions and not particularly roomy. Drivability, ride and roadholding standards were all excellent, and, despite the car being a little ponderous due to its weight, it certainly represented something of a breakthrough in improving small British saloons.

Solid and robust, the Y-type's chassis was soon to form the basis of future MG sportsters and, if not of spectacular performance itself, the Y-type could hold a high cruising speed. Late in 1948, the YT four-seat touring version appeared, slightly lighter and slightly quicker with its TC specification 1250cc engine. However, it was none too pretty and, much to the relief of most English MG enthusiasts, virtually all those produced were sent off for export. A more memorable Y-type derivative was the YB which appeared in 1951. It represented quite an advance from what was now the YA. There were 15in. (rather than 16in.) diameter wheels, a front antiroll bar, larger shock absorbers, a hypoid rear axle and improved brakes, all of which clearly improved the car's roadability. And like its predecessor, the YB wasn't against a spot of competition when given the chance. Despite their uninspired appearance, the Y-series cars reached a production total of well over 8000 (only 877 of these were YTs) by the time their end came late in 1953. With the TC Midget production figure rounding off nicely at 10,000, the days of true mass production had obviously arrived. Already ordered to produce Rileys as well as MGs, Abingdon had truly entered a new era.

MIDGETS GALORE

By far the most successful MG saloon to date, the Y-type continued in production until late 1953. Its running gear was to form the basis of the next generation of Midget sportsters

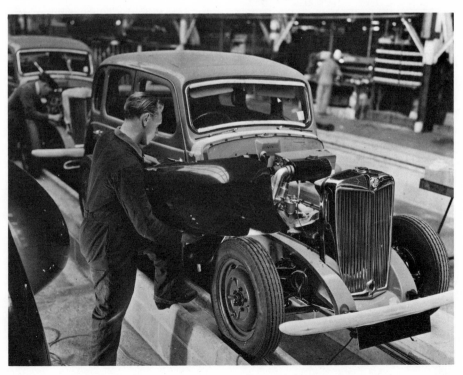

Based on a shortened Y-type chassis, the TD Midget caused quite a stir upon its introduction, its steel disc wheels creating the greatest fuss

In late 1949 MG's concession to Nuffield rule was the new TD Midget. The usual bunch of MG fanatics made their disapproval perfectly clear but, if the TC had captured hearts with landslide success, the TD, in almost trebling the TC's production figure, was to totally dominate the affections of sporting motorists.

"A coffin riding on four harps". "This petite bolide is in reality not an automobile, but a small coal-cart very cleverly disguised" - these had been just two of the comments applied to the TC by the American motoring press. And quite true they'd been, too, for despite the TC's mesmerising effect, innovation hadn't been one of its better points. Indeed, by 1949 demand was rampant for something a little more up-to-date than the TC's wrinkling pre-war design. Abingdon's answer was simple - the men just took a Y-type chassis, shortened it by 5 inches to the TC's wheelbase, and clothed it with an improved TC body. Thus the Midget now had rack and pinion steering and independent front suspension, plus, thanks to that suspension, four other trivial details that soon stirred up one hell of a fuss - the bolt-on steel disc wheels. The 1250cc, 54bhp. engine was exactly as it had been in the TC, but did improve in detail as production continued.

Although it closely resembled the TC, the TD had several distinct differences. For starters its body was four inches wider. Then there were the smaller 15 inch diameter wheels, the re-styled wings and the bumpers. Costing £569 with tax, the car was as rugged, abuse-resistant and tuneable as its forerunner. It also handled just as well, but did everything much more

comfortably. In 1950 (the first full year of TD production) Abingdon spewed out over 10,000 cars for the first time ever. Many of these were the TD, some the TD Mark II. This was officially a competition version of the TD, and had been prompted by a demand for more power; not a lot more - about 3bhp from a Stage II tuned engine. But there were such things as bucket seats and front suspension modifications - still not enough to attract the masses, however, for few TD Mk.IIs were built.

29,664 TD Midgets had been built by the model's end late in 1953; a staggering total, almost two thirds of which had gone to America. During its life this famous MG model, regarded by unbiased MG enthusiasts as the best of the T-series, brought back to life two old MG pastimes that had almost been forgotten since the war - factory sponsored circuit racing and coachbuilt derivatives.

Similar to the TC in appearance, the TD was a much more comfortable car to drive; a point appreciated by the Americans

Following his record-breaking successes during the two immediate post-war years, Goldie Gardner had tired of the Nuffield Organisation's very limited assistance. But changes on the Cowley board had finally sanctioned MG participation in record-breaking once again. During 1949 and 1950 Gardner and a variably engined EX.135 achieved enough records to make them the world's fastest partnership on four wheels in no less than five out of the ten International record classes. These were great achievements, but during 1951 and 1952 the weary projectile began to show its age with several failures beginning to appear amongst the further records gained. During 1952 one of the attempts at Bonneville Salt Flats,

TDs on the line. This model was regarded by unbiased enthusiasts as the best of the T-series cars

Utah, USA saw EX.135 spin and Gardner receive a bad knock on the head. His health suffered such that doctors persuaded him to retire. But by that time MG racetrack activity was gaining momentum once again.

George Phillips, Ted Lund and Dick Jacobs had driven works TC Midgets in English events during 1949. This had led to the trio piloting TDs during 1950, an outstanding result being their winning of the Team Prize for the first three placings in class in the T.T. that year. Le Mans wasn't forgotten, with Phillips gaining a 2nd in class in his TC 'special' fitted with light, self-made bodywork. For Le Mans 1951, Abingdon's old-established urge to achieve racetrack success obviously lived on - the factory decided to sponsor Phillips by building him a TD with a difference. Of basically the standard chassis and running gear, plus a tuned TD engine, the car was clothed with a graceful aerodynamic body designed by Sydney Enever who had been with MG since the first days at Abingdon. With a low frontal area to its all-enveloping open bodywork, and registered UMG 400, the MG prototype proved very fast at Le Mans before being forced into retirement by engine trouble after three hours. Despite any disappointment, the new machine had shown a promise that was to reach fulfilment within four years, in the revolutionary form of the MGA.

In 1952 came the first outstanding MG achievement on an American racetrack. With a highest overall placing of sixth, an MG team of three TDs scooped the Team Prize at the first ever Sebring 12 Hours Race in Florida.

During the early fifties MGTDs

The TF Midget was designed as a blend of traditional and modern styling elements

Introduced at the 1953 Motor Show, the TF's somewhat dated lines caused considerable disappointment amongst enthusiasts eager for a break with tradition

gave enormous pleasure to racing drivers both professional and amateur in many corners of the world. But it couldn't be denied that the car's angular open body was already very dated. Thus these years saw several attempts at rectifying matters by the established coachbuilders. Of course many enthusiasts had already turned to building their own home-designed MG 'specials', but rarely did these have the style of such as the Arnolt MG. Produced only in small numbers by S.H. Arnolt of Chicago, with an attractive GT style body designed and built by Italian stylist Bertone, the Arnolt MG was a luxurious four seater that soon became a collector's item. Also in the USA were such MG specials

as a stretched four seater saloon version of the TD. All these MG derivatives inspired greatly varying comment. It was ironic that the one TD derivative to inspire almost universally adverse criticism should come from MG themselves.

The car in question was the TF Midget which aimed at succeeding the TD with a blend of traditional and modern styling elements. The now huge numbers of MG followers found that aim unquestionably misguided! But sad to say, MG aims were no longer simply the inspirations of Abingdon, the decisions of Cowley. Following an important motor industry marriage in 1952, the Nuffield Group and the Austin Motor Company were now, as BMC, one and the same. Unfortunately for MG, Lord Nuffield had handed control over to Austin's number one - Sir Leonard Lord, the very same hardline businessman who had ousted Cecil Kimber as MG's managing director back in that fateful year of 1935. Lord had later resigned from his position with Nuffield, but now here he was back again with a tight grip on the reins of both Cowley and Abingdon. By the time of the TF's announcement, that grip had already proved fateful for one particular Abingdon-inspired aim that stemmed from the TD-based prototye that George Phillips drove at Le Mans in 1951.

Following the race a road-going prototype had been prepared, emulating the racer's attractive lines but featuring a new chassis which would seat driver and passenger lower in the body. Code named EX.175, the prototype was, in Abingdon's view, ideal as the outdated TD's successor. But late in 1952 Lord had already agreed that Austin should mass produce Donald Healey's Austin-Healey 100. Strict economist as he was, he saw no need within BMC for any sporting MG other than the old-fashioned traditional TDs. Furthermore, only the stark reality of MG's plummeting sales in 1953 persuaded him to sanction the TF.

As already stated, the TF caused considerable disappointment upon its debut at the 1953 Motor Show. It was minimally more modern than the TD, making concessions only with a forward sloping bonnet line, a sloping radiator, headlamps grafted into the front wings, a more sharply raked tail and individual bucket seats to replace the one-piece seating unit of the earlier car. In all other respects the TF was merely a TD with the 'competition' TD Mk.II's 1250cc power unit. Reflecting little more than token gestures, the windscreen could still be folded flat and wire wheels could once again be fitted as an option. Including tax, the TF cost £780 (representing an advance of £20 on the TD's price), upon

payment of which the customer received what was really an unhappy compromise. Producing 57bhp at 5500rpm, the engine didn't even allow very fast motoring. Eventually, in mid-1954, this led to the TF receiving what was known as the XPEG engine, a 1466cc unit developed from the most recent bout of record breaking.

Endowed with 63bhp at 5500rpm the TF1500 was a respectably quicker car than its older twin, and did at least keep MG competition activities alive. Despite the great derision heaped upon it by the motoring press, the TF's unusual and striking appearance was approved of by many during its short, 18 month lifetime, and later looked back upon with great affection - affection so warm that during the seventies some fairly close replicas would be produced. Based on Triumph chassis, the indifferent Spartan and the faithful RMB Gentry were both to be produced in reasonable quantities. But the MG enthusiast would not be fooled. For him the last of the square-rigged MGs was the TF, a comfortable little sportster that matured well with age. Only 9600 examples were produced at Abingdon, the model having become something of a stop-gap, though not initially intended as such. Sir Leonard Lord might originally have vetoed the 1952 MG EX.175 prototype, but by early 1955 he had at last seen the light. Before the exciting new model was born, however, MG had chalked up their latest medium-sized saloon. It had shared the 1953 Motor Show stand with the TF. In enthusiasts' eyes, the two cars had not made a happy pair.

Just like the sales figures for the open two-seaters, those for the MG Y-type had fallen alarmingly in 1953. To stop the rot and ultimately become easily the best selling MG saloon to date, the ZA Magnette entered produc-

Not quite but nearly – the TF's long term effect was such that it was the subject of some masterful forgery twenty years after its introduction. This is the Triumph-based RMB Gentry

tion at Abingdon at about the same time as the TF. It was received with very mixed feelings - hardly surprising in view of its badge engineering. The ZA was little more than a Wolseley 4/44 with an MG radiator and a new BMC 1489cc B-series engine. MG enthusiasts were again horrified. Their cries of anguish would have been far more impassioned had they known that the Z-series were to be the last MG saloons to be produced at Abingdon.

As a basic Nuffield design, the ZA's body/chassis unit was of monocoque construction, a first for MG. The front suspension was by wishbones and coil springs, while the solid rear axle rode on half-elliptic springs. The new engine was a conventional four cylinder effort producing 60bhp at 4600rpm - one not initially liked at Abingdon, but soon to demonstrate versatility and reliability via its enormous tuning potential. Easily outperforming its Y-series predecessor, the ZA was also given to some excellent roadholding, and later dis-

The Z-type Magnette, first example of badge-engineering under BMC rule. Needless to say, the die-hards were horrified!

played both abilities to good account with commendable results in International rallies and production car racing. With a sumptuous interior, it offered luxury car comforts at economy price. Despite the initial doubts, the car was a great success. Continuing in production until 1956 when the improved ZB Magnette appeared, the ZA had hit right at the heart of the ever increasing market for a robust responsive saloon with sporting pretensions.

While the ZA was doing an excellent job demonstrating the advantageous combination of Abingdon ability and BMC resources, Sir Leonard Lord had strangely enough sanctioned MG's return to a familiar pastime - record-breaking. Captain George Eyston had reappeared at Abingdon in 1953 with Lord's go-

Above: ZA Magnette production at Abingdon. Z-types were the last MG saloons to be built there
Below: Endowed with excellent roadholding and great tuning potential, Z-types were very competitive in racing during the mid-fifties. In 1977, too, as demonstrated by Judith Anderson's ZA in a classic saloon race

ahead to make another record run at Utah. The conveyance built by the factory for this attempt was based around a second chassis that had been produced along the lines of that for the EX.175 prototype. With streamlined bodywork and a new XPEG 1466cc engine (developed from the 1250cc XPAG unit), the new racer was code named EX.179. It was August 1954 when Eyston at last sat in the cockpit at Utah awaiting the 'off'. Incredibly, the car broke seven International and twenty five American National records over varying distances. Highest speed attained was 153.69mph with American racing driver Ken Miles at the wheel. There was obviously plenty of fire in the MG name yet.

It was early 1955 when the last of the square rigged MGs rolled off the Abingdon production lines. As it turned out, the TF had become something of a stop-gap. Though a great many MG followers would have had the

Latter day classic saloon racing again – this is Anthony Scott-Andrews' Varitone Z-type

traditional theme continued into the next model, it seems unlikely that tradition would have rescued MG's falling sports car sales. By now demand for ZA saloons far outstripped that for the TF. More and more sporting drivers wanted a motor racing background linked to their road-going sportsters. The likes of Jaguar, Aston Martin and Ferrari were already producing sleekly efficient sports cars and it was obviously time for MG to depart from the Midget tradition - a long line of cars that had changed less in outward appearance than virtually any other model over the same period of time. Several months of mid-1955 saw Abingdon without a sports car to build. But behind closed doors, and in the wings, plenty was happening.

Even when stationary EX.179 managed to look as though it was winding itself up for more record attempts. It was easily MG's most successful record breaker

BREAKING WITH TRADITION

In every facet of its character, in many details of its construction, the MGA heralded a whole new phase of MG history. The previous chapter has already noted this revolutionary MG's origins in the special bodied TD that ran at Le Mans in 1951, and in Sydney Eneer's EX.175 prototype of late 1952. The XPEG-engined EX.179 record-breaker of 1953 was also closely linked to the new car. Before the MGA's launch, Abingdon's love of code numbers was to manifest itself with yet another example, EX.182, the three cars built being even more closely related to the expected new-comers.

The EX.182s were officially racing prototypes. Indeed, with their aluminium bodies, luggage boots occupied by huge fuel tanks, passenger seats panelled over and tiny streamlined screens provided for their drivers, the cars differed considerably from their soon-to-follow road relatives. But to the public at large, the three racers were merely competition versions of brand new road cars, the association between their June 1955 Le Mans debut and their future as production cars being an MG master-stroke capably eliminating most of the expected fuss over what was a radical change from tradition.

The Le Mans outing was successful, if tragic. Powered by a developed version of the new BMC B-series 1489cc engine, as introduced in the ZA Magnette saloon, the three racers proved respectably fast. Sadly, the race was marred for all enthusiasts by the disaster of a Mercedes-Benz leaving the track, ploughing into a crowded spectator area and killing over eighty people. Both this, and the bad crash of Dick Jacobs' EX.182, somewhat overshadowed the success of the MG debut, but the two remaining cars finished a very satisfactory fifth and sixth in their class. Later the

81

An aerial shot of post-war Abingdon.
The main production lines were, and
still are, housed in the large block in the
centre of the picture

A new image for the world's most famous sports cars came with the outstandingly attractive MGA. Wire wheels were optional

same year a three car team competed in the Ulster T.T., two of the cars powered by experimental twin-cam engines. Again the results were very gratifying but, most ominously, again the event was marred by a horrifying accident. Tragic as they were, these accidents exaggerated the element of danger in motor racing. This had the unwelcome effect of ending once again the MG works teams' participation in competition. However, at least the new MG's high speed reliability had been well proved - just the ingredient needed for a successful launch. As it turned out, the demand for the new car was quite staggering.

With almost unnerving ability, MG had once again come up with a perfect formula. Making a fresh start

alphabetically after thirty years of rather confusing type letters and numbers, the new car was publicly announced in September 1955 as the MGA. Outstandingly attractive for its time, the open two seater steel body shape was to become a durable classic. In standard tune, the BMC B-series 1489cc engine (adopted, no doubt, largely thanks to its easy worldwide serviceability) initially gave 68bhp at 5500rpm, later being raised to 72bhp without increasing engine speed. The independent coil spring and wishbone front suspension system was closely related to that of the TF Midget, while the half-elliptic sprung rear axle followed that of the ZA Magnette.

'Safety Fast' was a slogan that could most certainly be applied to the MGA. 60mph could be reached in what was then a 'mere' 15 seconds, and the maximum was around 95mph, from which speed the car's 10in. drum brakes could slow it capably. Handling

was excellent too, and these general driving characteristics soon gave the MGA an enviable reputation. Bolt-on steel disc or centre-lock wire wheels could be fitted and everything about the car was just right, except, perhaps, its price - £894. In much the same form (not forgetting the wind-cheating 100mph hardtop coupé version of 1956) the inaugural MGA model continued right through until early 1959. No less than 58,750 examples were sold, of which just under a quarter were built in the first full year of production (1956), while a great percentage crossed the Atlantic to the USA. As predictably as ever, the drastic new ground broken by the MGA's modern styling greatly displeased MG traditionalists, but it quite obviously delighted a whole new generation of sports car enthusiasts the world over.

While the MGA was happily furthering the MG tradition, the ZA

1956 saw the introduction of the MGA fixed head coupé. One of the benefits was 5mph extra

Magnette saloon was coming to the end of a life during which it had done much the same thing, albeit in a rather different market. 1956 was well advanced when the ZA gave way to the ZB, the major change being the power unit, which, as it did in MGA form, now pushed out 68bhp at 5500rpm, thanks to a raised compression ratio and larger SU carburettors. Capable of 90mph, the ZB was the fastest 1.5 litre saloon available in Britain at the time, a point which it made perfectly clear in 1958 by winning its class in the BRSCC saloon car racing championship. The ZB also featured several interior detail improvements over the ZA, and was itself improved styling-wise with the Varitone model. This had a two-tone colour scheme and a larger, wrap-

This modified MGA was still looking good in the 1970s

round rear window. 1959 might well have seen the ZB distinguish itself further in competition, had it not been phased out - not without some regret. Like so many MGs, the Z-series had been introduced to howls of disappointment, yet had evolved into a thoroughly capable and much admired car. 36,600 examples were produced in all.

Between 1954 and 1958 Z-series Magnettes and MGAs performed creditably in all manner of competition work. Following the Le Mans and Ulster T.T. tragedies of 1955 the factory opted out of backing circuit racing and the emphasis reverted to rallying. Naturally the two models proved themselves as successful as ever. The circuits were not entirely deserted by MGs, however, a multitude of privately owned cars continuing to fly the flag with dignity in many countries. And there was still the record breaking, of course - another MG tradition that refused to lie down. Exactly two years after its August 1954 records at Utah in the hands of Eyston, EX.179 was back again, re-engined with one of the twin-cam units that had powered an MGA in the 1955 T.T. Once again many existing achievements were laid waste as sixteen new International class records were established that month.

The following year MG were at it again! Same place, same car, but once again a different engine - a 948cc pushrod ohv unit that was to end up later in the first Austin-Healey Sprite. First with supercharging apparatus, then without, EX.179 fairly flew through a whole host of International and American National records. Yet this was only the tip of the iceberg, for 1957 was little more than two-thirds gone when Sydney Enever's latest ground missile was unveiled - EX.181. This was quite a monster. Within its tubular chassis was a single forward-mounted seat and a mid-mounted supercharged version of the twin-cam 1.5 litre (basically B-series) engine that had done so well in 1956. Standard

MG front suspension and steering were fitted, while the rear end featured a de Dion axle with quarter-elliptic springs. The most startling thing about the whole car was its highly aerodynamic teardrop-shaped body with driver's vision through a diminutive glass canopy fronting a long, slender central bulge that tailed off with a single fin.

Following intensive development, the supercharged twin-cam 1489cc engine was showing output of no less than 290bhp. Thus it was that in August 1957 Stirling Moss and EX.181 joined the MG record breaking team by smashing five International Class F records with an average top speed of 245.6mph across the Utah Salt Flats.

EX.181's amazing speeds were

Powered by a supercharged 1489cc twin-cam engine, EX.181 was MG's last and fastest record breaker, achieving 245.64 and 254.91mph with Stirling Moss and Phil Hill driving respectively

With 108bhp on tap from its enlarged B-series engine, the MGA Twin-Cam was a fast if cantankerous machine

due mostly to its very refined version of the BMC B-series engine. Enlarged to 1588cc, though in somewhat milder form, the same engine was to be found in mid-1958 under the bonnet of the new high-performance MGA, the Twin Cam. Power output of the twin ohc unit was now 108bhp at 6700 rpm, driving through a close-ratio gearbox to new centre-lock steel disc wheels. The effect was enough to transform a rapid car into an extremely quick if cantankerous and problematical car. Only 9 seconds were needed before 60mph showed up, and the maximum speed was now 115mph, the sort of performance which definitely needed the Twin Cam's set of four disc brakes. The only adverse effect of all this performance was the understanding and attention needed to maintain it, for

such high efficiency did not take kindly to neglect. Not only that, but the revs came so freely that if the driver failed to keep a constant watch on his tachometer, he could easily dismantle the engine in rather shattering and unconventional style.

With typical MG ease, MGA Twin Cams took happily to the racetracks. The many results gained included an impressive first four places in class in the 1959 Silverstone GT race, and Autosport Championship class wins in 1959 and 1960 - not forgetting impressive class results in the Sebring 12 Hours for the same two years. One very individual Twin Cam racer was the special 1762cc engined fastback coupé built at Abingdon from the remains of one of the 1955 Le Mans prototypes for a private entry at Le Mans in 1959. No more than a nineteenth hour retirement was achieved that year (when sheer bad luck saw the car hit an Alsatian dog at over 100mph on the Mulsanne straight!), but the following year the same car did considerably better. Driven by Ted Lund and Colin Escott, it averaged 91.1mph to win the 2 litre class, a notable victory that unfortunately came only after the model had been discontinued (early in 1960). The Twin Cam's end had been signalled by the road car's general unreliability, its unfortunate habit of breaking down having created much bad feeling, particularly in the USA. Just over 2000 examples had been built by then. Well before the Twin Cam's end, however, another MG variant had established itself in the guise of the MGA 1600.

Compared with its T-series ancestors, the MGA had been a far more comfortable and convenient car to use daily. It had given fair fuel economy, fine roadholding and high speeds. However, during the late fifties motor car performance was progress-ing by leaps and bounds, and by spring 1959 the standard MGA's 1489cc engine was the subject of demands for increased performance. Accordingly, the unit's capacity was enlarged to equal the Twin Cam's 1588cc, bringing a useful increase in power output to 80bhp at 5600rpm, plus added low speed torque. After four years of MGA 1500 production many small improvements had been made, though this didn't stop many more being incorporated in the 1600. These included changes to the weather protection, braking, rear lights and pedal layout. So agile was the 1600 that before long several examples were in service with various British police forces overseeing law and order on the roads. The strong arm no doubt appreciated their rapid manoeuvrability and the ease with

More power, revised braking and improved comfort were offered by the MGA 1600

Timeless elegance has made the MGA 1600 something of a classic

which they could catch other vehicles! Both two seater open and coupé versions were still available, of course.

Such was Abingdon's reputation for settled, large quantity production that late in 1957 BMC's insensitive board had given the MG factory the unenviable task of building Austin-Healeys as well as MGs. By mid-1958 this task included construction of the new small sportster, the Austin-Healey 'frog-eye' Sprite. But one BMC car that MG were not expected to handle (no doubt much to their relief) was, strangely enough, an MG - in name if not in character. It was the multi-purpose, Pininfarina-designed, Austin A60/Morris Oxford monocoque body/chassis unit, designated, much to even the least volatile MG enthusiast's disgust, the MG Magnette Mk.III. Indeed, as the ZB Magnette's replacement, the undistinguished machine was no more an MG than it was a Wartburg! Its only MG components

were the 1489cc engine, gearbox, rear axle and instruments. It certainly didn't share typical MG standards of sporting style, good handling, fine roadholding and excellent performance.

BMC might have been happy with their latest piece of badge engineering but it certainly did the MG image no favours. Looking just like several other badge-engineered BMC plodders, the Magnette MK.III quickly eroded the MG's respected position in the sports saloon market. Whereas the ZB had been a lean, taut machine with a slightly vintage 'feel', the new car appealed to a whole new 'ordinary man's' market, albeit with a roomier, more comfortable interior, lighter steering, enormous boot and improved

Basically a Morris Oxford with an MG badge, the last of the Magnettes was hard pushed to match its earlier sisters' fine sporting reputation

visibility. Naturally enough, the 'ordinary man' quite liked the car's completely superfluous, stylist-dictated tail fins. Yet despite its mediocrity, the Magnette Mk.III sold almost as well as its much-loved predecessor. At the 1961 Motor Show it was displayed in somewhat improved MK.IV form with 1622cc engine and many detail changes. In carting thousands of family motorists about, it somehow continued in production until 1968. Abingdon had, and wanted, little to do with it.

Back in the land of more normal MG matters, Abingdon had followed the early 1959 MGA 1600 launch by pulling the dust sheets off EX.181, in which Stirling Moss had travelled so rapidly in 1957. With its 1498cc engine enlarged to 1506cc, it now made, in September that year, MG's last ever record run. To celebrate the occasion, it also made MG's fastest ever speed - 254.9mph in the hands of Phil Hill. The Abingdon expresses Had certainly progressed by leaps and bounds since EX.120 first broke records in DeceMBer 930.

By 1960 the Abingdon factory was something of an exception to the BMC rule in that it was mid-way between a fully-automated mass production plant and a handbuilt specialist car factory. About 1200 staff were employed, with John Thornley at the helm guiding such key men as Cecil Cousins, Reg Jackson and Sydney Enever. Building thousands of Austin-Healey 3000s and Sprites in addition to MGs, the men showed an extraordinary enthusiasm and willingness to continue the age-old MG 'atmosphere'. There was undeniably a kick to be received from constructing machines that discerning drivers would cherish and treat as an extension of their characters. Oddly enough, this was exactly what was happening with the well-out-of-date T-series MGs, for a great renaissance of interest in them had already made itself obvious. It would go on doing so, too, despite the appearance of the MGA 1600 Mk.II in Spring 1961.

Readily distinguished by an unusual, recessed radiator grille and other minor styling changes, the latest MGA was powered by an almost entirely new 1622cc engine providing an appreciable increase in power output (to 93bhp at 5500 rpm), which made itself most obvious when the car was cruising at high speed. Structural body improvements were also made, while both wire wheels and fixed head coupé options remained popular. A further option was the little known 1600 Mk. II De Luxe model with a pushrod engine in its slightly different all-disc braked Twin Cam chassis, but despite their pleasant characters, few of these models were ever made.

Without a doubt, the MGA model in all its previous guises represented everything that a good sports car stood for - good performance, confident and safe handling, endearing style, reasonable practicality and youthful character. It also kept the two famous initials at the head of the sports car design table, and did as much as, if not more than, any previous model in making them synonymous with the very term 'sports car' - at least in the mind of the vast majority of the general public. So many owners of conveyances even remotely resembling sports cars (whatever the marque) must have been regularly irked by the 'is it an MG?' question! But, in an increasingly modern world where consumers were subject to the ideas of ever-brighter marketing departments, even the MGA was already becoming old-fashioned. Indeed, at a time when the sports car market was changing its priorities fairly radically, the model

Above: This revised grille easily distinguished the MGA Mk.11 1600
Below: Seen from the rear, the Mk.11 1600 was readily distinguished by its new tail lights

Displaying somewhat mild modification and mild suggestion in 1976 is Rob Haigh's MGA club racer

which had prised masses of MG followers away from previous tradition was certainly no youngster during its seventh production year (heaven knows what critics of the day would have said some sixteen years later upon seeing the MGA's successor more than double that production life figure!).

What was happening during the early sixties was that saloon cars (even such as the diminutive Mini) were becoming an increasingly better match, handling and performance-wise, for their sporting counterparts. Emphasising the demand for liveliness with full practicality were the plummeting MGA sales figures of 1960 and 1961. Surprising though it may seem, at the time when, in spring 1962, the 100,000th MGA was completed at Abingdon to establish a sports car production record, the passing years had seen the model become decidedly basic when placed in a context of

everyday use. Just over a thousand further examples were built before the line finally rolled to a halt in June.

With automobile design taking ever greater steps forward, the MGA's successor would not only have to be thoroughly modern, but would also have to pull out all the stops to worthily replace an exceptional machine. The American market, which had gobbled up the large majority of MGA production, probably awaited the newcomer more anxiously than any. It was to appear at the 1962 Motor Show at Earls Court. Few could have guessed just how long MG fortunes would have to rely on both the next model and its smaller sister, the new generation Midget announced in June 1961.

THE SIXTIES-
A BRIGHT
ENOUGH
START...

Throughout their history the MG company had proved themselves gifted with a unique ability to adapt to the ever-changing patterns of sports car development. At no time was that talent more necessary than during the gestation of MG's two new sports cars for the sixties. As if it wasn't worrying enough to sports car producers one and all that saloon cars were rapidly reshuffling their basic concepts to close the overall performance gap appreciably, the BMC Mini had appeared in 1959 to lay down a whole new set of saloon roadholding standards. Further ground for ulcers

ADO 34 was one of Abingdon's lost causes. With a Mini engine under its bonnet, and thus front-wheel drive, it was proposed in both open and closed form

appeared when the Mini's already excellent power to weight ratio was given extra substance by the lively Mini-Cooper Mk.I and its 55bhp 997cc engine, as introduced in August 1961. This little bullet's announcement, and the subsequent appearances of its increasingly powerful sisters, were to have a far-reaching effect on sports motoring.

Indeed, the Mini-Cooper Mk.I itself was quick to make its presence felt on the Abingdon development staff. Naturally enough, upon the Mini's birth in 1959, they'd immediately enthused over its possibilities as the basis for a new small sports car. Within twelve months they'd built just such a thing. But while long drawn-out discussions were taking place over its production potential, the Mini-Cooper idea was proving itself quite obviously a much cheaper alternative within more or less the same market. So Abingdon's ADO.34 project, as it was known, was quietly extinguished, the concept being left to the open arms of a thriving band of specialist concerns. Their efforts produced such front wheel drive Mini-based machines as the Mini-Marcos and the Mini-Jem, and such rear-drive derivatives (the engine and sub-frame turned through 180 degrees and rear-mounted) as the Deep Sanderson, the Cox GTM and the Unipower GT.

Though deprived of its latest brainwave, Abingdon was already extremely busy handling production of all Austin-Healeys - as had been directed by the BMC hierarchy in 1957. Much of this work concerned the tremendously successful Austin-Healey Sprite, occupying just the market that MG needed to break into once again. Accordingly, while they were designing the completely new Sprite Mk.II that was released in May 1961, the MG men kept one further trick up their sleeves. One month later, they played it, and not to universal appreciation! The problem was that few MG enthusiasts knew of Abingdon's design involvement on the the latest Sprite, and when the brand new Midget was seen, to all intents and purposes, to be a very transparently disguised Sprite, their delight at the re-emergence of this much loved MG name was somewhat subdued. But despite the apparent duplication, and the diluting effect of this latest piece of badge engineering, the new Midget was another success story in the making - though with a little more of a struggle than usual, thanks mainly to the afore-mentioned Mini-Cooper.

If the MGA had broken the square-rigged body tradition, the Midget was responsible for breaking MG's separate chassis construction tradition in using a pressed steel monocoque-type body. Extremely rigid, this structure was fitted with wishbone and coil spring suspension at the front and quarter-elliptic springs for the rigid rear axle. 46bhp at 5500rpm was available courtesy of the slightly underpowered 948cc BMC 'A' series engine with twin 1 1/4in. SU carburettors, only enough for maximum speeds in the upper 80s and acceleration to 60mph in a surprisingly lengthy 20.2 seconds. Weighing just under 14cwt. and with a wheelbase of 80in., the Midget was an appreciably smaller car than the MGA, yet still managed to offer reasonable luggage space and good comfort for two (the cockpit's rear shelf could be used for children or small/very uncomfortable adults if the optional seat cushion was fitted).

Available with or without a detachable hardtop, the Midget's bodywork was smooth and attractive for its time, and differed from the Sprite only in its grille, minor styling

details and trim. Its introductory price was only £689, very cheap but still dangerously dearer than its closely related opposition. In their road test *The Autocar* saw the Midget as: "... approaching the ideal for the market which it is intending to serve." Certainly, with constant detail improvement, it was to become a very popular small fun car, despite the Mini-Cooper's equally rapid improvement.

Thanks to the Midget's common sense economy of sharing tooling and development costs with the Sprite Mk.II, Abingdon's development men must have been allowed that important extra time they required to concentrate on the somewhat more important MGA replacement. If a thoroughly modern and practical MG sports car were needed to maintain MG's position at the top of the sports car league, then the new MGB, as announced at the 1962 Motor Show, was certainly it.

Sharing its lines with the Austin-Healey Sprite Mk.11, the little 948cc Midget for the sixties soon became a very popular, albeit basic, fun car

The important thing was that within exterior dimensions appreciably less than those of the MGA, except in overall width, the MGB offered far greater interior space, and thus practicality, (particularly as it enjoyed wind-up glass windows in place of the MGA's primitive side-screen set-up). Bearing a strong family likeness to the Midget, the newcomer's integrally constructed bodyshell had, nevertheless, lost much of the MGA's classic grace in featuring stiffly parallel lines with large and fairly flat front and rear panels. Conversely, it had a confidently heavy and solid air about it. Access, the driving position and outward visibility were all excellent.

Bored out yet again, the poor old

Looking much like a scaled-up Midget, the MGB offered far greater interior space plus creature comforts like wind-up windows

BMC B-series engine was now of 1798cc, and much easier to get at than it had been in the MGA. Though power output of 95bhp at 5400rpm wasn't significantly higher than the MGA's figure, torque increase over the old 1622cc unit was no less than 13.4 per cent, thanks to a bottom-end redesign. Weighing 18.5 cwt, the MGB could reach 60mph in about 12 seconds and a maximum of just over 100mph, enough to quench the performance thirsts of the vast majority of sports car pilots. Looking fundamentally the same as those of its predecessor, the MGB's suspension, steering and brakes did incorporate a number of developments. The outcome was some typically confident handling, plus the retention of all the old MGA joy -

without the draughts and wind noise! This effortless mile-eater was announced at £950.

MG's two new offerings certainly looked capable of carrying them through the sixties in style. While the MGB was delighting its owners, the Midget was soon given a 1098cc engine (55bhp at 5500rpm) and disc front brakes to place power and braking efficiency more in keeping with the times. Also added was greatly improved interior trim, and the 0-60mph time was down to 16.4 seconds. In line with BMC's policy of constant improvement, detail changes (including the offering of a fibreglass hardtop and optional overdrive) were made to the MGB in 1963 at a time when the car was coming into widespread police use - even policewomen used to drive them for certain traffic patrol duties.

One 1962 offering that wasn't necessarily going to further the marque in real style was another unwelcome piece of badge-engineering. It was the octagon-adorned version of BMC's front-wheel-drive, hydrolastic suspension 1100cc saloon. Albeit a revolutionary MG, this machine must have made MG enthusiasts wince when they saw it advertised as: "The most advanced MG of all time"! Though the 1100cc range, with various BMC badges on their radiator grilles, were to enjoy several years as the United Kingdom's best selling car, the MG version, hardly surprisingly, could never be considered a tearaway success. Available with a two or four door body, the MG 1100 was notable for providing very generous interior space within quite a small package. The unique rubber cone suspension system gave a quiet smooth ride, and allowed surprisingly agile sports-type handling. For a complete change, a transverse front engine drove the front wheels. Capable of

87mph maximum and 50mph in about 15 seconds, the MG, with 52bhp at 5500rpm on tap, had slightly more urge than its BMC sisters. However, despite being an excellent all-round package, it was hardly going to arrest the detrimental effect this insensitive badge-engineering was having on the MG reputation. It had been started by the Magnette Mk.III, which was still in production at this stage as the Mk.IV. Ironically, only four days after the 1100 model was announced, Dick Jacobs entered one in the 6-Hour Saloon Race at Brands Hatch for drivers Andrew Hedges and Alan Foster, and saw it win its class comfortably. Another example was to fare well in the 1963 Monte Carlo Rally, but by this time MG were on the way

The octagon-adorned version of BMC's 1100 saloon was, in fact, an excellent driver's car, though never greatly loved by MG enthusiasts

to losing, once and for all, their previously well-respected position in the sports saloon market.

With the Midget and MGB models under their belt, MG were now well set for the sporting sixties. Constant detail improvement would see the cars maintain their reputations with ease. Upon announcement, the MGB had received some marvellous support from the press, with comments such as: "Unquestionably the best sports car ever made at Abingdon" and "The best engineered, the best put together MG we've ever seen". Not surprisingly, it sold rather better than the Midget; in fact it encouraged Abingdon to achieve several production records. An important factor here was the USA's widespread acceptance of the 'B'. Detail changes during 1964 and 1965 involved the car's engine (changing from three to five main-bearings), dashboard gauges, fuel tank and propshaft. The Midget, too, was receiving its fair share of attention. Spring-time 1964 saw it revitalised as the Mk.II (the Sprite keeping pace as the Mk.III) with engine power uprated to 59bhp and the rear suspension changed from quarter-elliptic to semi-elliptic springs. These changes kept it bang up-to-date performance-wise, so it was only fitting that styling was attended to with a new curved windscreen, and creature comforts were improved with better instruments, winding glass side windows, hinged quarter lights and lockable doors with externally operated press-button handles.

Above all a comfortable and totally practical sporting carriage (though it lacked the fire of some of its competitors), the MGB also grabbed its share of competition success in racing and rallying. Now settled in premises at Abingdon, the BMC competitions department had already squeezed huge rally success from the 'big Healey', and followed that up with widespread race and rally success for the works Mini-Coopers. Such positive results naturally encouraged a renewal of greater activity on the MG front - with the BMC management's guarded approval. Some of the earliest products of this were the three handsome aluminium-bodied coupés built on Midget bases at Abingdon early in 1962. With modified running gear, two of these cars soon became known as the Dick Jacobs Midgets, such was their success under Jacobs and his drivers, Alan Foster and Andrew Hedges. For some time now the American MG importers had been entering (and paying for) a team of works-prepared cars in each year's Sebring 12 Hours event. With varying success, this effort included MGBs as, indeed, did a remarkable return to Le Mans in 1963. With an extended, aerodynamic nose, fibreglass hardtop and tuned engine, this car, in the hands of Paddy Hopkirk and Alan Hutcheson, won its class at an average of 92mph despite a longish delay embedded in the sand at Mulsanne!

In 1964 another hardtop MGB, that of the Morley brothers, won the GT category in the Monte Carlo Rally, while Paddy Hopkirk returned to Le Mans, this time with Andrew Hedges and a similar extended nose car to his previous year's mount. The 99.9mph average attained wasn't high enough for a class win, but still saw the MGB in as first British car home. In 1965 further good results came from MG excursions to the Sebring 12 Hours, the Targa Florio, Le Mans (the Hopkirk/Hedges 'B' finding itself somewhat aged compared to its competition, but still finding the steam for a second in class), Phoenix Park (where MGs won the first five places) and Brands Hatch. This latter outing

Above: Paddy Hopkirk and Andrew Hedges drove this aerodynamically-developed
MGB to 2nd in class and 11th overall at Le Mans in 1965
Below: In GT form, the MGB became something of a poor man's Aston Martin, and
opened up a large untapped market in which it found instant success

was a 1000 mile race split over two days, and won at 75.2mph by Warwick Banks' and John Rhodes' MGB.

Whether or not the ever-quickening pace of life had already aged the MGB by 1965 was hard to say but, even so, a fall in demand was noticeable that year for the first time. True to form, Abingdon had the answer. It was a car that attracted a whole new market - the MGB GT. Sharing the open roadster's specifications, the GT used the same bodyshell from the waist down, but above it sported a fixed head, new larger windscreen and a large upward-opening, raked tail-gate on concealed hinges. The overall effect was very attractive indeed, and to the MGB's established sporting prowess was now added a new dimension in practicality - estate-type access to the flat rear luggage deck, and a folding rear bench seat that could be used for two small children. Costing a total of £998, the GT was almost 2cwt heavier than its open sister, but capitalised on its improved aerodynamics by having virtually the same performance. Again due to the new superstructure, suspension was stiffened and thus roadholding improved. Announced in October 1965, the new model was a rapid success, both at home and in the USA.

Apart from a couple of major engine transplants still to come, the MG range now settled into a somewhat depressingly monotonous pattern of mere regular detail improvement. For the 1966 Motor Show the Midget gained a new folding integral hood and 1275cc propulsion offering 65bhp at 6000rpm, 60mph in 13 seconds, a maximum of 95mph and Mk.3 designation. The pleasant if uninspiring MG 1100 also featured the occasional change, and even the dull Magnette Mk.4 was soldiering on in there somewhere.

After both the 1966 and 1967 competition seasons had proved variably entertaining for an assort-

Without losing any sporting appeal, the GT's opening rear door added estate-type practicality

Above: Following its acquisition of an 1100cc engine, wind-up windows and Mk.II designation in 1963, the Midget gained 1275cc power and a fold-away hood in Mk.III form

Below: Its nose having reverted to more familiar form courtesy of Abingdon's competitions department, the Hopkirk/Hedges '65 Le Mans car was raced again during 1966 and '67, including a visit to the Targa Florio

More power, an improved interior and the removal of its tail fins identified the 1967 MG 1300. The MG 1100 Mk.2 looked identical

ment of works MGs, the 1967 appearances of the MG 1300 (an 1100 with 1275 cc engine producing 58bhp at 5250rpm) and the MG 1100 Mk.2, both with tail fins removed, new rear lights and trim changes, were both strongly overshadowed by another re-engined MG. Its birth lay partly in the need to replace the 'big' Austin-Healey 3000, which was sagging sales-wise and in any case looked like an insurmountable barrier in the face of approaching American motor pollution legislation, and partly because of a revival of the large engine theme that had followed the MGB's original development - without fruition. Indeed, during the MGB's gestation various power units had been considered - the six cylinder 'C' series

engine, as used in the 100 Six and 3000 Mk.1 Healeys, amongst them. Then, when during 1963 the largest BMC sports cars were again under review, consideration was given to a V8-engined MGB. In the event, it was the much improved Healey 3000 Mk.3 that was to appear in 1964, but the big engined 'B' wasn't forgotten. It appeared at last at the 1967 Motor Show, a machine the Abingdon engineers were not wholly overjoyed with.

During 1967 BMC and Jaguar merged to form the short-lived British Motor Holdings, the MG Car Company becoming the MG Division. Continued rationalisation saw the approval of plans for a new 3-litre saloon complete with a substantially revised (at Longbridge) version of the old C-series engine. For obvious reasons, it was this engine which now propelled the new MGC. As the 'big' Austin-Healey 3000 was withdrawn during 1967 to leave a considerable gap in the large engined sports car market, the MGC was naturally seen as an attempt to fill the breach. Unfortunately, things misfired rather badly.

MG's new generation Healey 3000 was announced at the 1967 Motor Show amidst an atmosphere of high expectancy. Its engine, the first with six cylinders since 1939 and the largest ever in a production MG, was similar to that of the Healey 3000, but featured a new block with no less than seven main bearings crowded into a rather inadequate length of crankshaft. Of 2912cc, the unit delivered 145 - 150 bhp at 5250rpm, a healthy enough sounding figure. But the gremlins had already edged in during development - arriving from Longbridge, the engine had proved heavier and taller than expected. The additional weight called for a complete redesign of the floorpan's forward half to include a triangular structure accommodating torsion bars in place of the standard coil spring layout. The work involved was probably rather more complicated than Abingdon had hoped. A direct result of the new engine's height was the wide bonnet bulge that became the C's trademark and readily distinguished it from the otherwise almost identical MGB. MGB rack and pinion steering was retained, and all-synchromesh gears were now standard, automatic transmission being optional (exactly as offered on the MGB that same October).

Clearly, MG hadn't tried very hard to make the MGC visually more exciting than its predecessor - it did have new door handles and wheels one inch larger in diameter and rim

After dabbling with big-engined prototypes during the mid-sixties, MG finally came up with the 6-cylinder MGC in 1967. It wasn't the fireball that fans had hoped for

Only larger wheels and a wide bonnet bulge distinguished the 'C' from the 'B'. This lack of separate identity didn't help sales

width, but these hardly increased its appeal. Available at £1102 as an open roadster and £1249 in GT form, the car was nevertheless very reasonably priced and one of the fastest-ever MGs. The drawback was the way the power was delivered. A maximum of around 120mph was fine, and acceleration fast if not dramatic, but the engine's lack of low speed torque and reluctance to rev loudly broadcasted the lack of exactly the ferocity the car badly needed. Other criticisms that came to light in a series of remarkably unenthusiastic road tests by the motoring press concerned the gearbox, heavy fuel consumption, general lethargy, heavy steering, huge steering wheel and, perhaps worst of all, a strong tendency towards understeer.

The general onslaught was probably the harshest MG had ever experienced. After comments such as 'gutlessness and pig-like understeer', the only praise to soothe the car's hurt pride referred to its smooth ride and refined cruising ability.

Much more of a high speed touring vehicle than a sports car, the thoroughly disappointing MGC had, somewhere in the vast workings of BMC, completely lost the 'Abingdon touch'. Consequently, though it was excellent fodder for the attentions of tuning concerns, and was even used by the usual assortment of police forces, it never sold well. It did, however, sire a very exciting racing derivative. Following the MGB GT's class win in its first major event at Sebring in 1967, the BMC competitions department were suitably encouraged to order six lightweight aluminium MGC GT bodies. Ordered before the production MGC's announcement, these bodies,

106

This unlikely MG 1100 was built in 1966 by Doug Wilson-Spratt. With a standard floor pan and aluminium coachwork, it remained a one-off

with their pronounced wheel arch flares and faired headlamps, looked mean and hungry, and it was a pity the standard cars didn't at least share their brutal and exciting image.

The disappointing outcome of those six unique bodies was that only two were ever completed as works racers. Using a standard steel floor-pan and an MGB engine bored out to 2004cc to provide 150bhp, the first one finished 9th overall in the 1967 Targa Florio. Re-engined with the intended 2912cc 'C' series engine (modified to give over 200bhp), the same car finished a very creditable tenth overall in the 1968 Sebring event, before being joined by the second works car for the Nürburgring 84-hour Marathon. The results here were less creditable, with one retirement and one sixth place (despite this car, the original one, being out of action before the race's end). While

In 1967 Doug Wilson-Spratt rebodied an early MGB racer with very pleasing results. It made a unique road and race car, and was even the subject of (eventually unfulfilled) plans for limited production

these very special works racers showed clearly that the inherent drawbacks of standard MGCs could easily be overcome, no further action was taken and the pair were sold off to America, the four other bodies, still unused, being sold privately. Three of them later made very desirable 130mph road cars.

Towards the end of the sixties a great change appeared to have come over Abingdon. Thanks to an American lawyer named Ralph Nader, all sorts of demands were now placed on the MG development men, including regular crash-testing under strictly controlled conditions and enough exhaust pollution work to warrant the construction of a fully-equipped £60,000 laboratory. It was hardly surprising that production suffered as a consequence, though soon revived. itself again to the extent that more MGs were produced in 1969 than in any previous year. Important here was that exports to the USA were now running at a high level. But the dilution of the MG 'atmosphere' had been increasingly evident - the departure of competitions manager, Stuart Turner, had indicated its downhill slide from its one-time position as a force to be reckoned with; there was the demise of the 'big' Healey and the MGC

Above: This business-like machine is one of the lightweight MGC GTs built by John Chatham, and raced by him at the Targa Florio in 1970

Left: Apart from being a competitive racer – it is seen here in the hands of Chris Drake waiting for the 'off' in a post-war historic car race at Silverstone during 1977 - VHY 5H also made a very desirable 130mph road car

debacle; a certain regret that the Midget was no longer the cheap and simple sports car it had set out to be; after nearly 50 years service Cecil Cousins retired; the coming of a mere MG division under the British Motor Holdings set-up; the fact that the lightweight MGCs were the last MG works racers; and last but not least, after the ever-growing influence of Longbridge under the BMC regime, the takeover of British Motor Holdings by Leyland, an old-established manufacturer of commercial vehicles. It seems almost irrelevant to report that somewhere in the midst of it all, Abingdon hardly noticed the final phasing-out of the old Magnette Mk.4 (accompanied by the MG 1100 and the four door MG1300).

The dilution of MG's unique 'atmosphere' by the growing influence of BMC during the late sixties had little effect on the continued popularity of the MGB

FADED MAGIC AND COMMERCIAL LOGIC

Despite the continued volume production and great popularity of the Midget, MGB and MGB GT, by the late sixties a certain rot had unswervingly eroded the old-time MG 'atmosphere'. During 1968 there was considerable uncertainty at Abingdon, a sense of insecurity that gnawed away at staff from boardroom level to apprentice fitters. Under the collective title of British Leyland Motor Corporation, the new masters of the Leyland/BMH merger were busy looking at rationalisation. It was of no encouragement that MG's main rivals in the sports car market, Standard-Triumph, had already been swallowed by Leyland, and were now under the same wing.

Continuing the apparent decline came the end of all BMC's house magazines, including 'Safety Fast', the withdrawal of support for BMC car clubs, including the MG one, and Sir Donald Stokes' statement that the

competitions department would be increasingly restricted, and would concentrate on racing saloons anyway. Then, in further BLMC rationalisation, MG were saddened to learn of their grouping with the Austin-Morris Division outside the more exalted Specialist Car Division. After some poor health general manager John Thornley now retired, and was followed by many of the longer serving employees who strongly resented the continuing deep upheaval. With the sudden closure of the Abingdon competitions department in August 1970, the factory's 'certain something' was generally reckoned to have been extinguished once and for all – sadly a triumph of matter over mind. Strangely enough, production continued to rise steadily.

Announced in October 1968, the MG1300 (available recently in two-door form only) for 1969 had reached Mk.2 designation with a considerably

111

After the MG 1100 Mk.II and the MG
1300 had been phased out, MG's saloon
fortunes rested solely on the two-door
1300 Mk.II of 1969

uprated engine giving 70bhp at
6000rpm. Performance was thus
improved, and the whole interior
received a facelift. With MGC production eventually petering out late in
1969 after 4542 open roadsters and
4457 GTs had been built, it was now
left to the ageing MGB and MGB GT
models to uphold the MG name.
Surprisingly enough, they looked like
doing the job capably, despite increasing signs of the open version's seven
year old wrinkles. But while MG
enthusiasts were wondering just what
delights might be in store with the next
model from Abingdon, a depressing
series of detail face-lifts were all they
were to get – unexciting changes like
the new front grille, new seats and
new wheels offered at the 1969 Motor
Show; equally uninspiring (but
necessary) improvements to the heater

and to the open car's hood at the 1970
Show. Though the B and BGT models
had capably followed the general
trend towards refinement and
habitability, eager critics knew they
were becoming a little long in the
tooth. Indeed, some interesting factory
prototypes were in existence around
this time, and were being considered
as possible 'new era' MGs. One of these
renewed an idea that could already be
traced back some ten years.

In 1960, soon after the Mini's
announcement, a further Issigonis
project was a front wheel drive sports
car based on the long wheelbase Mini
estate floor pan. The plot was to offer
examples with open or closed fastback
bodywork, and MG or Austin-Healey
badges. That idea and the existence of
a prototype were extinguished by the
arrival of the new Midget of 1961, but
in 1970 Longbridge was seriously considering for the Abingdon production
lines another machine of similar
layout. Coded as ADO 70, this car was
based on a Mini 1275GT taken from

112

Still game for action, John Sprinzel and Gerry Ryan's MGC GT is seen here on the 1970 Monte Carlo Rally

the original production batch late in 1969. With the Mini floor pan, running gear and Hydrolastic suspension remaining as standard, its steel body was fashioned at the Turin workshops of Michelotti. It was an attractive little car, and not unlike the soon-to-be-announced Fiat X1/9 in its practical concept – two seats and two removable Targa roof panels. The second, and even more exciting, MG prototype was an all-new (apart from the power unit) mid-engined sports car using de Dion rear suspension. Sad to say, it was kept very hush-hush and never proceeded from the prototype stage.

Despite its obvious promise as a truly modern and practical Midget replacement, ADO 70 died in the face of the large amounts of money that were needed to see it through growing and severe legislation from the USA. After a year during which Syd Enever had retired and MGB production had reached the 250,000 mark, the 1971 Motor Show produced the same old story – MGB and Midget. The Midget's constant sales superiority over the Sprite had seen the latter phased out during the year, a technical victory which the small MG was possibly celebrating with a new, larger fuel tank and, for the American market, a detuned pollution-regulated engine. Another car which passed away

Miss MG, 1971, poses with the 250,000th MGB. A left-hand drive model with the new recessed front grille, it went to the USA

during 1971 was the MG1300 Mk.2. Leaving Abingdon concerned only with sports cars (for the first time in many years), this last MG saloon had, oddly enough, gathered itself a fine reputation, for despite its badge-engineering it still enjoyed the good performance and excellent handling that MG saloons had once been so noted for. Through the various MG1100 and 1300 models, no less than 143,067 examples had been produced.

With a great many older MGs now becoming much sought-after classics, 1972's commercially-orientated staple diet of MGB and Midget showed how frustratingly

During the early seventies MG enthusiasts were beginning to wonder why an MGB replacement hadn't appeared. In fact, the EX.234 prototype had existed since around 1968. Adaptable for 1275cc and 1798cc engines, it could also have replaced the Midget!

predictable Abingdon's output had become, particularly for the most loyal followers of the marque. And even more particularly when an unchanged range was announced for 1973 at the 1972 Motor Show, with such inconsequential but loudly heralded improvements as a new BAS injection-moulded radiator grille, matt black windscreen wipers, new steering wheel, arm rests, new badges and cigar lighter! But following some experiments in 1967 when both 2.5 litre and 4.5 litre Daimler V8 engines had been planted under MG bonnets, 1972 did at least hold one promise in store. Rover had joined the group in the late sixties, and after some extremely prolonged development, several Rover V8-powered MGB GTs were running about that year. These first ever eight-cylinder MGs were finally announced to the public in August 1973, though only after Kent engineer Ken Costello had paved the way for quite some time

Above: Last new model to date is the MGB GT V8. Visually unexciting, its performance is another matter!
Below: Not much space to spare with the lightweight Rover V8 engine sitting in an area designed for half that number of cylinders

with his own private production line. The official Abingdon version was surprisingly scorned by some as just another British Leyland badge-engineered hybrid and not a true MG, but even so its sensational performance promised to install it as a very capable flagship of the fleet.

Available in fixed head form only, and not for export to America, the GT V8's aluminium engine was tailored for its new home with its carburettors re-mounted at the rear. Although the water radiator had been enlarged, two thermostatically-controlled electric fans were needed for cooling. With 137bhp on tap at 5000rpm (and almost double the torque of the four cylinder

The appearance of the Fiat X1/9 severely dated MG's image. Behind this 1973 Midget is a rear-engined Unipower GT, its design dating back to 1965 and posing the question; 'Why couldn't MG have done something similar?'

MGB), the casing of the all-synchromesh C-type gearbox was redesigned to accept a larger clutch, and the intermediate gear ratios raised. The standard MG unitary structure needed changes to its bulkhead, inner wheel arches and front cross-member to accommodate the five-bearing pushrod ohv unit, and while the front suspension remained unaltered, its rear counterpart gained substantially uprated springs to control the new found urge. The brakes also received attention, and a collapsible steering column was adopted for greater safety. But the most positive outcome of all this was the superb performance of 0-60mph in 8 seconds and a maximum of over 120mph from a car that cost a very reasonable £2294.

Where the V8 scored so handsomely over the MGC was in having a high output engine that was virtually no heavier than the iron 1800

unit. No longer was the large engined 'B' in constant danger of demolishing fences on fast bends! But one valid criticism was that the V8 employed the 1965 vintage MGB GT bodyshell. Sure enough, it was still a fairly attractive shape and was even distinguished in its new form by tinted glass, a door-mounted mirror and some new, very strong alloy and steel composite 5J rims. Once again, though, just as there had been upon the MGC's announcement, there was the strong feeling that this wasn't anywhere near enough. Likewise, the rather antiquated interior and great, unwieldy steering wheel weren't really in keeping with a brave new high-performance image.

While producing an excellent all-round sports car in the MGB GT V8, Abingdon had failed to come up with the outstanding recipe that would revitalise the drooping MG image right down at its roots, the sensational something that would unconditionally restore the magic of those two simple initials. Undoubtedly, exhaustive cash-consuming automobile regulations were showing increasingly less pity, and one mustn't forget that an output of less than 50,000 cars per year still made MG something of a specialist producer. But with the motoring press and thousands of MG fans constantly questioning the old MGs' continued validity, and sports cars like the superb (in almost all respects) Fiat X1/9 beginning its rampant success in Europe and America, time seemed to be running short. Amazing though it may seem, this was to be an ever-present feeling for some years hence. No answers were to materialise, yet strangely enough no detrimental effect was to be felt at Abingdon. Production simply continued to rise, and showed no signs of losing an enviable 80% going for export to America and Canada.

As already noted, the Mini and its Cooper derivative really set the pattern for huge improvements in saloon car handling and performance in the early sixties. By the seventies a great many two litre family saloons could more than match the MGB and BGT. The 1974 models made no effort to improve the situation. That year, while workmen were extending Abingdon's Air Pollution Control Centre, excavations revealed eight skeletons, believed to be over 1500 years old. Unfortunately no plans for replacing the MGB were found amongst the Roman remains, but the impending Motor Show did hold in store a few efforts at vandalising its appearance a little – not forgetting its stablemates.

The root causes of the latest (and horrific) changes were MG's reliance on US exports, and thus the need for continued compliance with American safety laws. For 1975 all MGs were to sprout ungainly and substantial front and rear bumpers designed to absorb the impact of a 5mph crash and then recover their normal shape. As if these didn't ridicule the dated bodyshells enough, their ride height was increased (the Midget by 1in., the MGB and GT by 1.5 in., and the already higher MGB GT V8 by 0.50 in.) to American order. This not only further lessened their sporting appeal but also adversely affected handling by producing excessive roll. Further changes to the MGB and BGT brought them into line with the BGT V8 – the fitting of a collapsible steering column together with corresponding column-mounted stalk controls and V8-type instrument pack (with smaller speedometer and tachometer), door mirrors, hazard warning lights and brake servo. Prices had now reached £1847 for the open MGB, £2101 for the BGT and £2795 for the BGT V8.

The most radical change made to

**Above: 1975 model MGs sprouted
monstrous 5mph crash impact bumpers
and rode higher on their springs
Right: No model was spared the
indignity of forced compliance with
American safety laws**

the Midget that October was its adoption of the four cylinder 1491cc engine as used by the Triumph Spitfire. Tailored to fit the MG by using a new exhaust manifold and air filters, and mated to an all-synchromesh Morris Marina 1.3 gearbox, the new power unit provided 65bhp at 5500rpm. Performance wasn't significantly improved but added torque gave better mid-range pulling power. The car's price was now £1351, and it remained a compact, practical and mildly endearing car to drive, particularly with women in mind. Forgetting that modern performance levels still left it with something of a struggle at times, 0-60mph in about 12 seconds and a maximum of just over 100mph were at least respectable. For the USA, all MG models were down on power due to their specially adapted,pollution-conscious and somewhat strangulated engines.

120

While the MGB GT V8 suffered from engine supply problems and the continued demand for its sisters proclaimed how best Abingdon's production capacity should be exploited, March 27th 1975 brought a notable company landmark – exactly fifty years, all of them very successful, had passed since the original registration of 'Old Number One'. Still thriving, and with 5000 members in the USA alone, the MG Car Club planned special commemorative events throughout the year. There was little hope of a dramatic new MG to encourage the celebrations, but Abingdon did chance its arm with a slight deviation from the norm. Certain of becoming a collector's item as only 750 examples were to be built, this was the Golden Anniversary MGB GT. Specially finished in British racing green and adorned with a full length side flash in gold, this model was equipped with such normally optional items as GT V8-type wheels, tinted glass, overdrive, head restraints and carpets. Along with all MGs produced during the anniversary year, its bonnet also featured a special gold MG badge.

Predictably though reluctantly, 1976 saw the final MGB GT V8s off the Abingdon lines. With 2800 examples built (at least one of which would have

greatly displeased any MG driver had they encountered it during the year — finished in anonymous orange, it was on surreptitious police duty as a 'plain clothes' traffic car), the space was now more usefully devoted to the four cylinder 'B's. True enough, they just kept on selling! Whether this was due to modest public taste or to the yearly updates was hard to establish, but needless to say the run-up to the 1976 Motor Show brought yet another batch of revisions. Both open and closed MGBs now received stouter front and rear anti-roll bars than the single item previously fitted to the GT only. The interior boasted a new facia with revised instrument layout, minor

**Only 750 examples of the Golden
Anniversary Limited Edition MGB GT
were built, thus ensuring its future
desirability**

switch and control changes, a smaller
steering wheel, column stalks as used
on other Leyland cars, full carpeting
and seats with built-in head restraints
and brightly striped nylon fabric trim.
Other improvements included halogen
headlamps as standard, modified
pedals and the fitting of a ther-
mostatically controlled electric fan. In
total there were no less than twenty
modifications, all combined in a united
attempt to shave the whiskers off what
the more irate MG enthusiasts were
now referring to, in correspondence
with the motoring press, as: "Two seat
Morris Oxfords"!

In two important areas, the 1976
changes improved the MGB and MGB

Produced in mid-1976, this Midget Special for the USA market had AM/FM radio, a special luggage rack and distinctive side stripes. Oh, well ...

GT a great deal. The new anti-roll bars just about eradicated the handling and roadholding deterioration introduced by the previous year's raised ride height, and the interior changes increased comfort no end. But to view the 15 year-old evergreen as a serious 1977 sports car in the more memorable Abingdon tradition simply wasn't on. By mid-1977 MG prices had rocketed – £2085 for the Midget, £2843 for the MBG and an unnerving £3576 for the MGB GT. While the prices were obviously not going to go down, power already had – from 95bhp to 84bhp. As *Autocar* said in its road test of the GT: "Outperformed in almost every respect by newer designs, it is fading quietly away in a shrinking corner of the market". The American magazine *Road and Track* had already been harsher: "Perhaps British Leyland will have the last laugh. The MGB could be the first replicar that never went out of production!"

Nostalgia, of course, had become an obsession on both sides of the Atlantic, and it is interesting to note that Abingdon's famed TC/TD and TF models were now most popular amongst the MGs being lovingly re-created in replicas built by enthusiasts. While the Americans built replica TC/TDs on none other than Volkswagen chassis, in Hinckley, Leicestershire, TF enthusiast Roger Blockley had found himself with a thriving business. Much as the TF was his dream car, his financial resources had dictated that the only answer was to build a very close replica on a Triumph Vitesse chassis. Little did he guess that plenty of other enthusiasts who weren't rich enough to pay the

124

Demonstrated by a British Leyland executive, this revised interior was the most noticeable change for the 1977 model MGB

A Midget transformed! Replacing the MG's ageing wrinkles with some traditional fun is the Arkley SS body conversion that has proved so popular through the seventies

original TF's current asking price would be just as happy with the next best thing. Accordingly, Blockley's RMB Gentry body kit soon found a big demand. From the early seventies, the modern Midget had also come in for its fair share of enthusiast attention, but in a rather different way. John Britten's sports car garage of Arkley, Herts, had devised a clever method of rebodying the car. Leaving the floorpan, doors, scuttle and running gear untouched, off came the front and rear bodywork to be replaced with traditional-style fibreglass panels. The result was a cheerful, almost cheeky appearance that rather suited the Midget's fun pretensions better than the original thing, and many hundreds of Arkleys have been built to date.

Like its bigger sisters, the standard Midget had withered badly by the late seventies. As an adequately lively open car, some of its original appeal was retained, but with a heavy price tag and a high insurance rating, its original aims of simple and cheap fun were lost forever. In Britain it soldiered on possibly because there was so little else on the market in its price range, but in the USA sales were dwindling. As *Road & Track* magazine had stated so bluntly: "Anyone who would buy a Midget when the Fiat X1/9 was available for only 1000 dollars more would have to be a complete masochist".

It is not pleasant to chart the MG marque's deterioration through the seventies. But the fact is that as each year makes a token attempt to supposedly revive the famous sports car with tawdry facelifts, Leyland, increasingly plagued with financial problems themselves, seem content to

let the MG magic fade away until it dies once and for all – taking the cars with it. Rumours, however vague, have certainly stretched as far as to suggest Abingdon's closure. Of course, it is fair to say that volume production cars today have to battle through a ludicrous legal obstacle course. True, development costs are continually inflated by the requirements of new legislation; true, the economics of it all are now unbearably frightening; true, the mandatory stipulations loaded on today's prototypes were undreamt of by yesterday's builders. But it's also fact that time does not stand still; that despite MG's efforts, progress cannot be halted.

The extraordinary paradox of it all is that MGs continue to sell. While Abingdon's workforce of 1180 men build a steady 50,000 outdated chariots per year, each and every one of them finds a ready buyer. Even the Leyland directors and the Abingdon

Barry Sidery-Smith at the wheel of the 1965 Le Mans MBG which was still as active as ever in club events during 1977

executives must be surprised at how they keep on selling. Perhaps this is because, thanks to a remarkable legend, the term 'sports car' is synonymous with MG more than any other marque. MG have weathered many storms through their history, and there is no reason to doubt that the MG magic will eventually be capturing motoring hearts once more. There can, however, be little excuse for complacency. The fact that the most experienced and respected critics have written themselves to distraction pointing out the inadequacies of current MGs, only to see their heartfelt words fall on stony ears, is surely a crazy monument to the dubious philosophy, "If it sells, why bother to replace it?" One wonders what Cecil Kimber would have thought....

Brands Hatch in 1977, and an array of Abingdon sportsters contest one of the regular MG Car Club events.

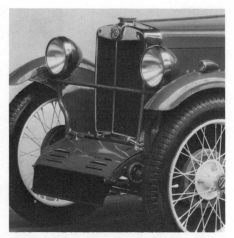

MGT222

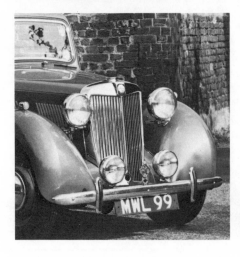

MWL 99

277 FJO

About the author

Best known for his work chronicling the hundreds of limited production specialist cars that have been built in this country since the last war, Peter Filby is now firmly established as a champion of 'alternative' cars. As the leading authority in his field, he is a popular monthly columnist in both *Hot Car* and *Motor*, and also contributes regularly to *Autocar, Thoroughbred and Classic Cars* and *Car Mechanics.*

Without attempting to be technical, his writing style aims at lively reading and an insight to the more human side of car manufacturing - characters, moods, situations and, above all, humour. Other books by the same author include *TVR - Success Against the Odds* (Wilton House Gentry) and *British Specialist Cars, Vol. 2 - Roadsters, Replicas and Fun Cars* (Bookstop).